Quebec Prehistory

## Canadian Prehistory Series

A growing interest in Canadian prehistory and the introduction of new archaeological techniques have resulted in significant discoveries across Canada. This series enables the general reader to enjoy for the first time a popular account of these exciting new findings in Canadian prehistory. Each book explores the prehistory of a particular geographical or cultural area and the authors, who are leading scholars in their fields, describe many fascinating aspects of archaeological research. Time charts, graphs, maps, and numerous photographs and drawings recreate a vivid picture of the life of the native peoples in Canada before Jacques Cartier.

Archaeological Survey of Canada
**National Museum of Man**
**National Museums of Canada**

# Quebec Prehistory

J. V. Wright

**Van Nostrand Reinhold Ltd.,** Toronto
*New York  Cincinnati  London  Melbourne*

Library of Congress Catalogue Number 78-60764

---

CANADIAN CATALOGUING IN PUBLICATION DATA
Wright, James V., 1932-
    Quebec Prehistory

(Canadian prehistory series)

Bibliography: p.
Includes index.
ISBN 0-442-29831-5

1. Indians of North America — Quebec (Province) — Antiquities. 2. Eskimos — Quebec (Province) — Antiquities. 3. Quebec (Province) — Antiquities. 4. Excavations (Archaeology) — Quebec (Province) I. Title. II. Series.

E78.Q3W75      971.4'004'97      C78-001594-0

---

Printed and bound in Canada by T. H. Best Printing Company Limited

79 80 81 82 83 84 5 4 3 2 1

Distributed in Canada exclusively by
Van Nostrand Reinhold Ltd.
1410 Birchmount Road
Scarborough, Ontario M1P 2E7

DESIGN: Brant Cowie/Artplus Ltd.

PHOTOGRAPHS: G. Barré (Figure 14), C. R. Harington (Plate 3), R. J. M. Marois (Plates 1, 2), P. Plumet (Plate 25), W. E. Taylor (Plates 19, 20, 21, 22).

COVER: About 2000 years ago, Dorset people carved a series of stylized faces in the soft bedrock near Wakeham Bay, west of Ungava Bay in northern Quebec. Although the specific purpose of these carvings is unknown, they probably express supernatural beliefs. To bring out the details for the photograph, red ochre was rubbed into the carved lines of the face.

To obtain the French-language edition of this publication, please write to the Publishing Division, National Museums of Canada, Ottawa, Ontario K1A 0M8.

Pour obtenir l'édition française de cette publication veuillez vous adresser à la Division de l'édition, Musées nationaux du Canada, Ottawa (Ontario) K1A 0M8.

# Contents

# List of Illustrations

## Colour Plates

## Black-and-White Plates

## Figures

## Maps

## Diagram

# Preface

The province of Quebec encompasses an area of 1 356 791 square kilometres, a land mass only slightly smaller than France, Spain and Norway combined. Within this area, there are great variations in both the nature of the land and the plant and animal communities that occupy it. In the extreme north, caribou graze on the arctic tundra, while whale, walrus, seal and polar bear inhabit the coastal waters. Most of the province is covered by coniferous forests spread over the rugged Pre-Cambrian rock of the Canadian Shield. Within these trackless forests are found moose, caribou, black bear, beaver and other smaller animals and an abundance of fish, such as trout, whitefish and pike. In southern Quebec, the mixed hardwood forests grow upon soils deposited by the glaciers or reshaped by the ancient Champlain Sea. The flat to rolling landscape is frequently broken by the massive bedrock remnants of the Appalachians. This region has been home to the white-tail deer, elk, black bear, moose, and a wide variety of smaller animals, fish and birds. Roughly separating the southern region from the harsh Shield country to the north is the mighty St. Lawrence River, whose lower reaches abound with whale, porpoise, seal, salmon, eel, capelin, and many other species.

Prehistoric peoples had to adapt to this great diversity of landscape, climate, and animal and plant communities. The earliest written records locate the Inuit along the province's northern coast and the eastern side of Hudson Bay, the northern Algonkian-speaking hunters in the forests of the Shield as well as along the north shore of the Gulf of St. Lawrence, and Iroquoian-speaking farmers in the upper and middle St. Lawrence River valley. The range of distinctive native cultures that have occupied Quebec can be seen in the prehistoric record despite major natural events, such as the last glaciation. Eleven thousand years ago, for example, early hunters could have occupied extreme southern Quebec, whereas as late as 5000 years ago portions of the northern Shield country had just been abandoned by the last

**Plate 1. Elevated Beachlines** View of the ancient beachlines north of Blanc Sablon on the north shore of the Gulf of St. Lawrence. Sea-level changes and coastal uplift have elevated the beaches well above the present sea level. This process has taken place gradually and, as a result, the earliest evidence of prehistoric human occupation occurs on the highest beaches. As one descends towards the sea, the archaeological remains become progressively later in time.

**Plate 2. Excavation within a Grid** This site at Lake Abitibi is being excavated with mason trowels within a carefully surveyed grid of excavation units. The process of excavation would destroy information unless accurate records were kept of the location, depth and associations of all objects. Drawings and photographs of profiles and floor plans are also necessary in order to reconstruct what happened at the site. Several thousand years of prehistory are often contained in only a few centimetres of soil.

remnant of the continental glacier. Subsequent climatic fluctuations have resulted in the shifting of plant communities and their associated animal species, including man. As if these and associated complications were not enough, the majority of Quebec is covered by acid soils that effectively destroy all bone, thereby depriving the archaeologist of a major source of information from an already severely limited data base.

Despite the magnitude of the problems facing archaeology in the province, a general picture of the prehistory of Quebec is gradually emerging. The picture is blank in certain areas, incomplete in others, and always blurred; such is and always will be the nature of archaeological reconstructions. Distorted and incomplete as it undoubtedly is, there would be no picture at all without the efforts of archaeologists working in the province. And this would be a loss, since Quebec's is a rich and fascinating prehistory. Jacques Cartier, Samuel de Champlain and other early European explorers and missionaries made many valuable observations regarding the native peoples of Quebec. What European observers could never learn, however, was when and how the Inuit came to reside in their present location, how long ago and from what direction man first occupied the province, when and where corn was first grown in the province, and whence it had come. These and a host of other questions can only be answered by archaeology assisted by other disciplines.

Because of its subject matter, archaeology is one of those fortunate studies that can, and indeed must, incorporate elements of knowledge from every discipline concerned with man and nature. This means that virtually all fields of human knowledge are applicable in one way or another to problems facing the archaeologist. The earth sciences and the biological sciences are particularly important. Physics and chemistry make direct contributions. Mathematics is essential to demonstrate certain patterned behaviour. The list goes on and on. Throughout the exercise, however, man is the primary subject under

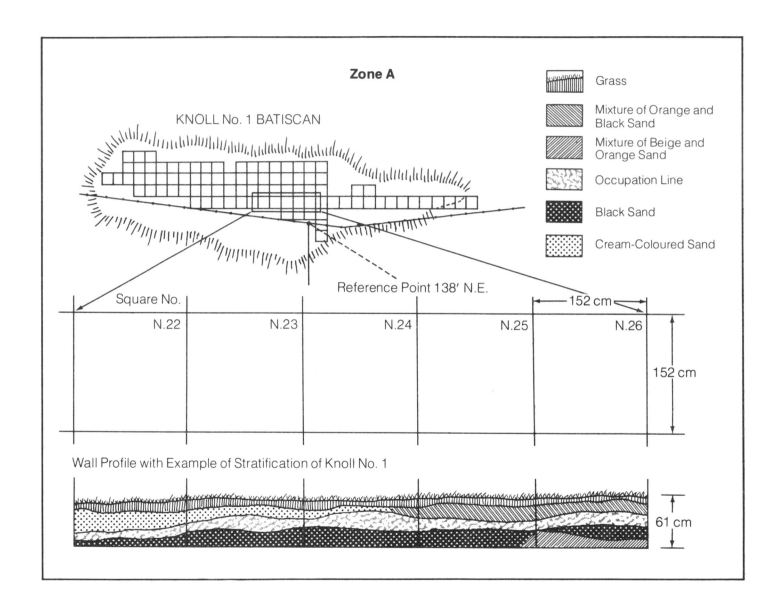

**Zone A**

KNOLL No. 1 BATISCAN

Grass

Mixture of Orange and Black Sand

Mixture of Beige and Orange Sand

Occupation Line

Black Sand

Cream-Coloured Sand

Reference Point 138′ N.E.

Square No.

N.22    N.23    N.24    N.25    N.26

152 cm

152 cm

Wall Profile with Example of Stratification of Knoll No. 1

61 cm

**Figure 1. Profile Record within a Grid System** Before excavating, the archaeologist lays out a grid system over the section of the site that he wishes to examine. Each square in the grid is given its own designation, and all information, artifacts, refuse, features, profiles, photographs, and soil samples are keyed to the square designations. This form of horizontal and vertical control of data is essential if the archaeologist is to obtain the maximum amount of information from his investigations.

investigation, and man has greatly complicated matters because his culture has, to a large degree, determined the ways he has adapted. Rigorous scientific method, then, is incapable of providing the total means for understanding man. There is an element of art in archaeological interpretation that must straddle the hazardous area between humanism and science. Given the subject matter, it cannot be otherwise.

Most of the archaeological work in Quebec has been carried out within the last ten years by professionals and non-professionals, who together have made substantial contributions to the province's prehistory. Graduate students, the professionals of the future, are also involved in excavating sites in the summer and analyzing the recovered data in the winter. This marked increase in archaeological investigation has resulted in the publication of a number of books and papers, most of which are technical in nature. But much information also resides in unpublished notes, monographs, and people's heads. This unpublished information, together with the technical publications, formed the basis for this book. By combining the evidence available from Quebec with that of the related prehistoric cultures of Ontario, Newfoundland, the Arctic, and New York State, it has been possible to outline the major aspects of Quebec prehistory. Unfortunately, large areas of the province have never been examined by an archaeologist, and other regions, such as the St. Lawrence estuary, have only recently been subjected to intensive research. Ongoing and future excavation will modify this synthesis, but hopefully most revisions will not radically alter the general picture presented here.

In a very real sense all syntheses are premature. The cumulative nature of information acquisition in archaeology ensures that such is the case with the present work. But "premature" is a relative word, since absolute maturity is unattainable. While fully acknowledging the limitations of the evidence upon which this reconstruction is based, I believe that the exercise serves a number of very useful purposes. First, it provides the interested public with a general archaeological outline containing many facts and observations that up to this time were known to only a small group of scholars. Second, the very process of reducing complex and frequently equivocal evidence to a form comprehensible to a general audience has made it necessary to rigorously appraise many underlying assumptions and to clearly recognize the weak areas in the reconstruction. In time, this synthesis will be replaced by a better statement on the prehistory of Quebec, which in its turn will also be replaced. Such syntheses are an essential element in the advancement of knowledge.

# Acknowledgements

My sincere appreciation is extended to the following scholars, whose critical reading of the manuscript resulted in constructive changes: Drs. R.J.M. Marois, G.F. MacDonald, and R. McGhee of the Archaeological Survey of Canada, National Museum of Man; Dr. W.E. Taylor, Jr., Director of the National Museum of Man; Dr. J.F. Pendergast, former Assistant Director (Operations), National Museum of Man; Messrs. C.A. Martijn and G. Barré of the Service d'archéologie et d'ethnologie, Québec; Dr. N. Clermont, Département d'anthropologie, Université de Montréal; Dr. P. Plumet, Section Histoire de l'art, Université du Québec à Montréal; Mr. J. Benmouyal, Saint-Lambert, Quebec; Mr. G. Samson, Centre des Études nordiques, université Laval; Dr. G.M. Day, Canadian Ethnology Service, National Museum of Man; and Dr. J.A. Tuck, Department of Anthropology, Memorial University of Newfoundland. Drs. Taylor, Marois and Plumet and Mr. Barré also provided illustrations, as did Mr. C.R. Harington of the National Museum of Natural Sciences. Thanks are also due to the Photographic Section of the National Museums of Canada and to Mr. D.W. Laverie, draftsman on the Archaeological Survey of Canada staff, for his excellent maps and drawings.

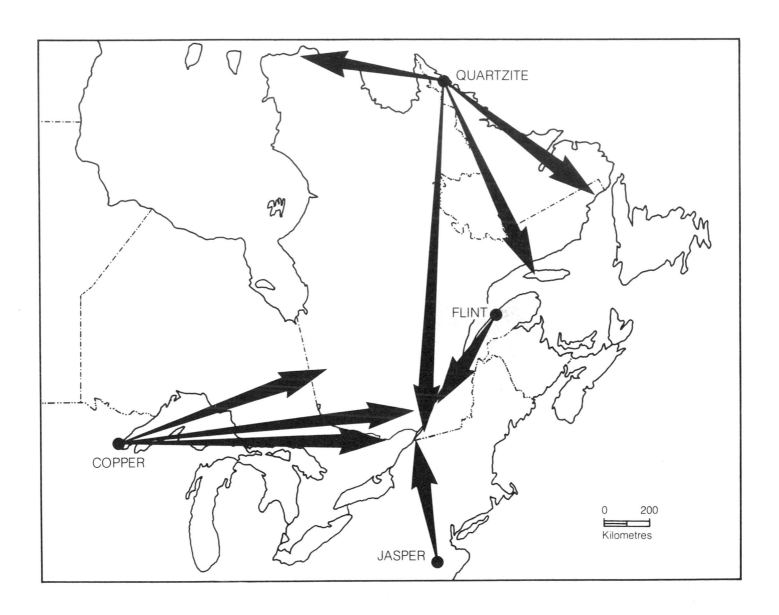

# Introduction

**Map 1. Prehistoric Trade Networks**
Circles indicate the geological sources of minerals, and the arrows point to the archaeological sites where material from these sources have been recovered. The actual routes the minerals followed to reach the sites would not, of course, be the straight lines shown on the map.

The prehistory of Quebec involves two distinct populations – the Indians and the Inuit (Eskimos). Although these two populations were occasionally in contact with each other, there appears to have been little interchange of ideas. Treating them here as separate units, therefore, is not an entirely artificial device.

The Indian prehistory of Quebec can be best discussed under three different physiographic regions: the hardwood forest region of the upper St. Lawrence River (including the Ottawa River valley) and the Eastern Townships, the Canadian Shield region of the north, and the St. Lawrence estuary. Prehistoric developments within these three regions are, for the most part, distinct from one another.

For convenience, the hardwood forest region will be referred to as the Southern Region. The prehistory of this area is closely related to that of southern Ontario and northern New York State. It is the only region in Quebec where agriculture was practised, and it was predominantly occupied by Iroquoian-speaking peoples in historic times. Similarly, the enormous tracts of the Shield will be called the Northern Region. Its prehistory is most closely related to that of the Shield region of adjacent northern Ontario, both regions being occupied by bands of Algonkian-speaking hunters in historic times. The St. Lawrence estuary will be referred to as the Estuary Region. This area appears to have been occupied from earliest times by populations that exploited its rich maritime resources. In historic times, Iroquoian-speakers inhabited the upper portion of the estuary, and Algonkian-speakers occupied the lower reaches. The populations of these regions did not live in isolation and there is evidence of wide-ranging contacts. In addition, climatic changes could favour the way of life of one group over another and result in the advance or retreat of cultures with different adaptations.

The Indian prehistory of Quebec will be considered under four time periods: the Palaeo-Indian period (9000 B.C. to 5000 B.C.), the Archaic period (5000 B.C. to 1000 B.C.), the Initial Woodland

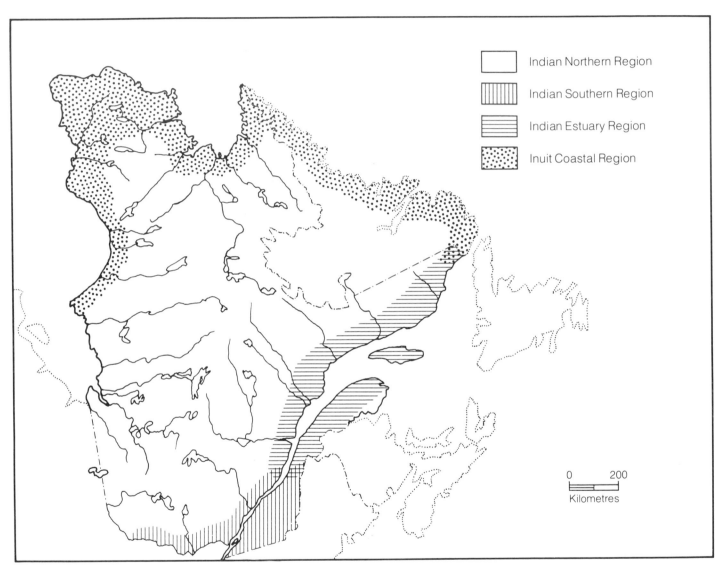

**Map 2. Archaeological Regions**

Legend:
- Indian Northern Region
- Indian Southern Region
- Indian Estuary Region
- Inuit Coastal Region

0    200
Kilometres

period (1000 B.C. to A.D. 1000), and the Terminal Woodland period (A.D. 1000 to the historic period). The Terminal Woodland period ends shortly after the appearance of European settlers, whose arrival initiates the historic period.

The Inuit prehistory of Quebec involves the east side of Hudson Bay, the northern coast of the province, and the extreme eastern portion of the north shore of the Gulf of St. Lawrence. It can be divided into two time periods: the Palaeo-Eskimo (2000 B.C. to A.D. 1450) and the Thule (A.D. 1250 to the historic period).

Time periods for both the Indian and Inuit prehistories are artificial devices used by the archaeologist to assist in the study of approximately 11 000 years of Quebec prehistory. It would be convenient to be able to slice up the time column into layers, which could then be described as separate entities; unfortunately, there are fuzzy areas between and within these major periods. Each, however, does possess certain characteristics that enable archaeologists to differentiate it from the others.

| Years Ago | Period | Southern Region | Northern Region | Estuary Region |
|---|---|---|---|---|
| 300 | | St. Lawrence Iroquois and Algonkian cultures | Algonkian cultures | St. Lawrence Iroquois and Algonkian cultures |
| | Terminal Woodland | | | |
| 1000 | | | | |
| | | Meadowood and Point Peninsula cultures | Laurel and Shield cultures | ? |
| 2000 | | | | |
| | Initial Woodland | | | |
| 3000 | | | | |
| 4000 | | | | |
| 5000 | | Laurentian culture | Shield culture | Maritime culture |
| | Archaic | | | |
| 6000 | | | | |
| 7000 | | | | |
| 8000 | Palaeo-Indian | Plano culture | | Plano culture |
| 9000 | | | | |
| 10 000 | | Clovis culture | | Clovis culture |
| 11 000 | | ? | | ? |

**Diagram 1. Chronological Chart of Quebec Indian Prehistory**

# CHAPTER 1

# The Palaeo-Indian Period
## (9000 B.C. — 5000 B.C.)

Two cultures that possessed different tools but followed a similar way of life lived in Quebec from approximately 9000 B.C. to 5000 B.C. The earlier Palaeo-Indian culture is called Clovis and the later culture is called Plano.

## Clovis Culture

Clovis culture is found throughout North America east of the Rocky Mountains, except in the areas of the continent that were covered by the glacier. The ancestors of the Clovis culture must have entered North America from Asia at a time when the two continents were connected by a broad plain, which is now submerged beneath Bering Strait. Indeed, these early hunters, following the game herds, would not have known that they were entering another continent. The uniformity of their culture over enormous tracts of North America suggests that the Clovis people must have spread very rapidly throughout the new land. Eventually, Clovis culture began to diversify as the various regional bands of Clovis people changed in response to local conditions.

The findings from a site in Nova Scotia suggest that Clovis culture occupied the northeastern regions of North America between 9000 B.C. and 8000 B.C. Only the extreme eastern and, more likely, southeastern parts of Quebec could have been occupied by man at this early date, as Map 3 indicates. Most of the remainder of the province was then covered by the continental glacier and the Champlain Sea. Although Clovis sites or tools have not yet been found in Quebec, sites and surface finds of the distinctive Clovis dart heads have been recorded in the Maritime Provinces and in the areas of Ontario, New York and Vermont adjacent to Quebec.

Most archaeologists believed until recently that the Clovis people were the first immigrants to the New World, and that their rapid expansion was due to the abundance of unwary game

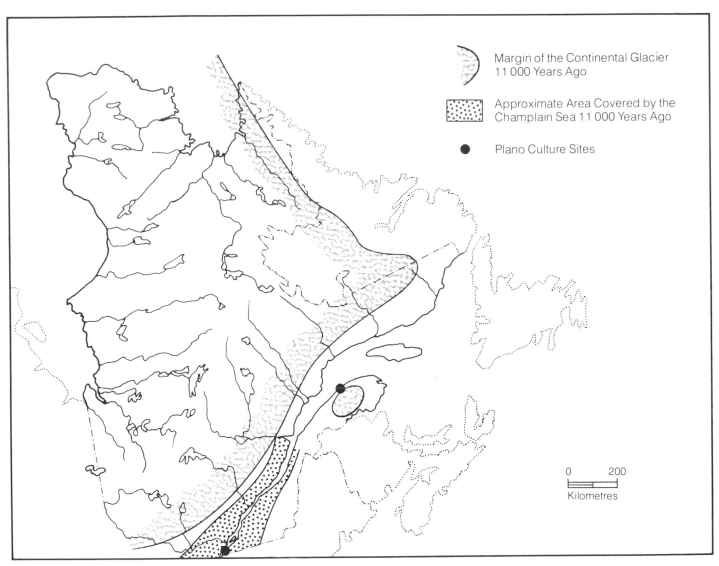

**Map 3. Palaeo-Indian Period**

Margin of the Continental Glacier 11 000 Years Ago

Approximate Area Covered by the Champlain Sea 11 000 Years Ago

Plano Culture Sites

0    200
Kilometres

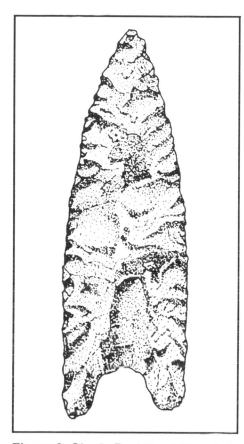

**Figure 2. Clovis Dart Head** Found at the 10 500-year-old Debert site in Nova Scotia. Similar points will likely be found in the Eastern Townships of Quebec at some future date.

animals and the lack of competition from earlier human occupants. However, new evidence from the unglaciated part of the Yukon Territory suggests that man lived there as early as 30 000 years ago. Some of these early people apparently drifted as far south as South America, where they established cultures that were markedly different from Clovis culture, yet of approximately the same antiquity.

The great number of later cultures that appear to have descended from the relatively homogeneous Clovis base can be simplistically divided into a western group and an eastern group. The eastern group is discussed in Chapter 2.

## Plano Culture

The western group, the Plano culture, developed on the high plains and adjacent regions. Although their penetration to the east was weak and incomplete, two areas of Plano occupation have been found in Quebec: one along the northern coast of the Gaspé Peninsula and the other on the islands in the upper St. Lawrence River. The age of the Gaspé sites has yet to be firmly established; the earliest available radiocarbon dating is approximately 6000 years. The island sites in Lake St. Francis cannot be much older than 9000 years, because the Champlain Sea covered the region only 9500 years ago.

The Gaspé sites contain natural deposits of stone that could be fashioned into tools. The sites, therefore, are characteristically littered with stone flakes, cores, and unfinished tools, broken or discarded during various stages of the manufacturing process. Knives, scrapers, drills, hammerstones, and iron pyrite nodules were among the tools found at one excavation. The nodules may have been used to start fires by striking them against a piece of flint to produce a spark. One of the dart heads from the upper St. Lawrence River area appears to have been manufactured from stone found in the Gaspé quarry sites. Should this be the case, there is a basis for suggesting that these early hunters possessed some form of water transport that enabled them to travel the 800 kilometres of river and sea separating the two regions. Projectile points from both areas possess the fine "ripple" flaking that is a marker of the Plano culture. The projectile points from Quebec, however, are different from related point varieties recovered from sites on the high plains. They are similar to a point found in New Brunswick and, to a lesser degree, to points from Ontario sites along the north shore of Lake Superior. This suggests that there may be a distinctive eastern variety of the Plano culture.

The continental glacier had shrunk considerably by Plano times, but the remaining ice and glacial lakes still greatly restricted the areas of the province that could be occupied. The Clovis and Plano people hunted large game, although in the Estuary Region the Plano hunters would certainly have exploited the rich maritime resources as well. The climate in Quebec during the Palaeo-Indian period appears to have been subarctic, and it is likely the major prey was the caribou. However, this does not mean that other food sources that assured survival would have been ignored. Palaeo-Indian man, like his descendants, would have had a carefully balanced set of seasonal rounds, ranging from berry and egg gathering to big-game hunting. We may assume that these people had developed the kind of clothing and shelter that enabled them to survive the severe climate.

Evidence of the Palaeo-Indian period in Quebec is very scarce. Not only were the populations undoubtedly small, but the physiography (climate, flora, fauna, bodies of water and drainages) of the occupied area was also substantially different from today. These differences, caused by the proximity of the continental glacier and its associated bodies of water, have severely complicated the archaeologist's search for excavatable sites. Acid soils and time have also combined to destroy all cultural

**Plate 3. Fossilized Capelin** This fossil, which is approximately 10 000 years old, was found in Champlain Sea deposits near Ottawa. The capelin is a small marine fish that occurs in arctic waters and is common today in the lower Gulf of St. Lawrence. During the spawning cycle, immense schools of capelin are attracted to sandy beaches, where the females lay their eggs; the males follow to fertilize the eggs. Incoming waves return the fish to water, although many become stranded on land and perish. During this vulnerable period in their breeding cycle, enormous quantities of capelin can be easily collected by hand. They are readily preserved by drying in the sun. The early Plano people of the St. Lawrence valley undoubtedly exploited this rich seasonal resource.

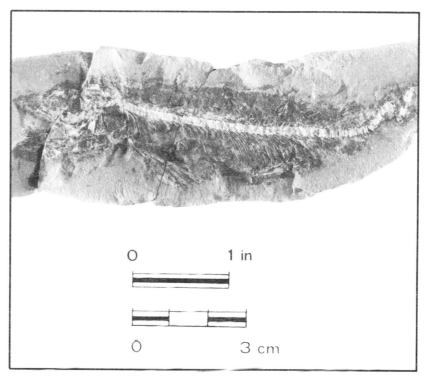

elements made from materials other than stone. As a result, the archaeologist must attempt to reconstruct the Palaeo-Indian period in the province from a small number of discarded and lost stone tools and the stone-chipping debris of quarry sites – surely a pale reflection of the total culture that must once have existed. Hopefully future investigations will locate Palaeo-Indian sites where such features as hearths, pits and tent floors can be excavated to enhance our picture of these peoples.

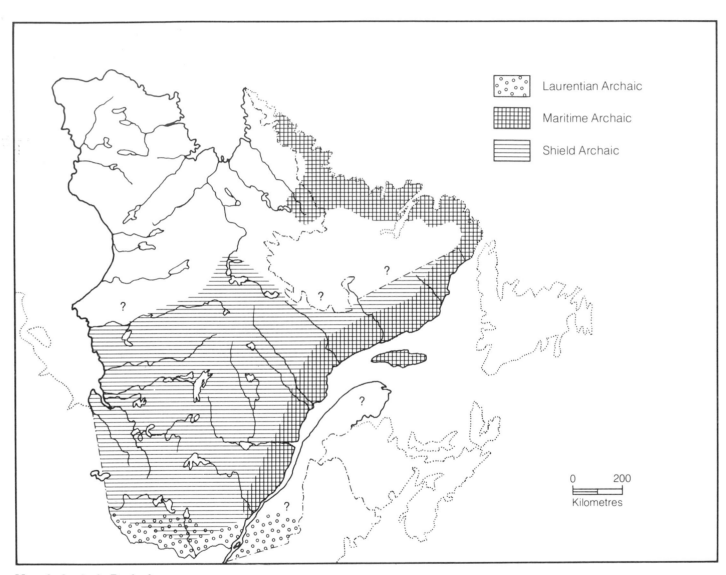

**Map 4. Archaic Period**

Laurentian Archaic

Maritime Archaic

Shield Archaic

0    200
Kilometres

# CHAPTER 2

# The Archaic Period
## (5000 B.C. — 1000 B.C.)

Three major Archaic cultures occupied Quebec: the Laurentian culture in the Southern Region, the Maritime culture in the Estuary Region, and the Shield culture in the Northern Region. The origins of these three cultures are somewhat different. Both the Laurentian and Maritime cultures may have developed out of the Clovis culture, although not in the same regions; the Maritime culture has always been oriented towards the sea, whereas the Laurentian has always been adapted to the interior hardwood forests. The Shield culture, on the other hand, appears to have evolved from a western Plano culture and to have gradually expanded eastward through the Shield country as the plant and animal communities reoccupied the land vacated by the retreating glacial ice.

None of these contemporaneous Archaic cultures lived in isolation. There is evidence of cultural contact, particularly along major rivers like the St. Lawrence and the Ottawa. But each culture was basically adapted to its own environment: the Shield people to the harsh regions covered by the Boreal Forest, where it was necessary to rely upon caribou and fish; the Laurentian people to the warmer climes and richer faunal and floral resources of the southern hardwood forests of the Great Lakes-St. Lawrence forest region; and the Maritime people to the St. Lawrence estuary with its rich maritime resources. The cultures were not restricted to the present political boundaries of Quebec. The Shield culture occupied the northern parts of Ontario and Manitoba and the southern Keewatin District to the west, and even penetrated into Labrador to the east. The Laurentian peoples lived in southern Ontario, northern New York and Vermont, and other sections of the New England States; and the Maritime culture occupied all of coastal Labrador and the island of Newfoundland as well as sections of the Maritime Provinces. The distribution of the three Archaic cultures shown on Map 4 is, of course, an approximation. Such maps are based upon the information available and are always subject to change in the light of new findings.

**Plate 4. Laurentian Artifacts**

**a.** Typical chipped-stone dart heads.

**b.** Two ground-slate dart heads on the left, and two native copper dart heads on the right.

**c.** Native copper fish-hook.

**d.** Sandstone abrader with notches at the top for attaching to a cord.

**e.** Native copper gouge, which served as a specialized adze.

**f.** Plummet of unknown function.

**g.** Polished slate spear-thrower weight (see Figure 3 for explanation of its function).

**h.** Possibly a bone dagger.

**i.** Ground-slate lance.

**j.** Stone gouge.

# Laurentian Culture

It is estimated that Laurentian peoples occupied the Southern Region of Quebec for more than 4000 years. The pattern of life during this time does not appear to have changed much until the introduction of agriculture. Populations seem to have been larger than those of the earlier Palaeo-Indian period.

Laurentian cemeteries in Quebec and adjacent New York have revealed that the people were of robust build. They suffered from bone fractures and arthritis, and their coarse diet frequently resulted in gum disease and tooth loss. Some of the remains indicated violent death: there are skull fractures, projectile points lodged in bones or the chest cavity, and headless skeletons. An unusual discovery from New York clearly indicates an unsuccessful surgical attempt to remove the tip of a projectile point from a human forehead. The oldest dated Laurentian skeletal remains come from Coteau-du-Lac in the upper St. Lawrence River valley. At this site, a human upper-limb bone was radiocarbon-dated at 4710 B.C. ± 145 (S-1154). (The ± 145 refers to the mathematical probability that the true date falls somewhere between 4855 B.C. and 4565 B.C., and the S-1154 is the University of Saskatchewan catalogue number for the date that was determined in their laboratory.)

Food bones found at the sites suggest that the Laurentian peoples relied upon big game such as deer, elk, bear and beaver. Smaller game animals, fish, shellfish, wild plants and other supplementary foods were also eaten. We can assume that a series of well-established seasonal rounds existed, consisting of fishing, berry picking in the spring through autumn, depending on the species, nut gathering in the fall, and trapping passenger pigeons and other migratory birds during their major periods of concentration in the spring and autumn. Men hunted big game while women fished or collected edible plants. Survival for short periods of the year depended upon some of the supplementary

**Figure 3. Atlatl Weight** The Aztec word atlatl refers to a specialized implement used for throwing a spear with greater force than was possible by hand alone. The atlatl was the weapon most feared by the conquering Spaniards, since spears propelled with this device could pierce armour. From 4000 to 2000 B.C. early hunters in eastern Canada carefully fashioned stone atlatl weights. Cylindrical holes were drilled through these by the bow-drill technique, even through a substance as tough as quartz. The weights were then attached to the atlatl shaft or throwing board to increase the force of propulsion.

The weight is attached to the shaft in this drawing. The atlatl (without the weights) was still in use among the Inuit until recently.

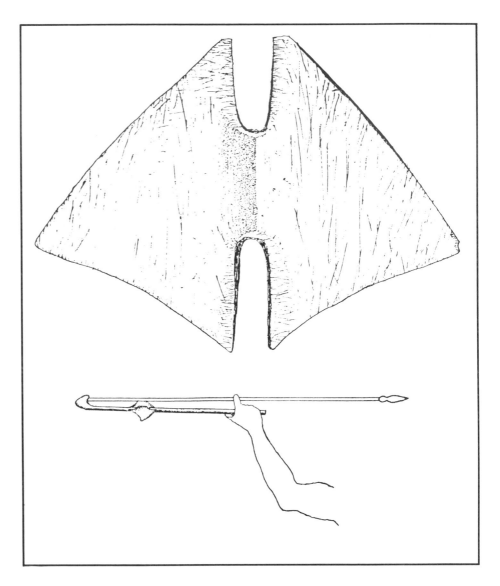

food sources. Without big game, however, the hunting bands could not have survived throughout the year.

Local variations in food resources were important. An area rich in spawning sturgeon offered an advantage over other areas. Extensive passenger pigeon nesting places, on the other hand, compensated for the absence of large fish. We can be fairly certain that people who were dependent upon animal foods for their survival were intimate with the behaviour of their prey and exploited their environment to the fullest.

Little is known of the houses used by the Laurentian peoples of Quebec. The majority of the sites excavated by archaeologists were summer encampments and the temporary structures that were probably built have disappeared. In addition, the climate was milder 5000 years ago, thereby reducing the need for protection from the cold. In the late fall, when families moved into the winter hunting grounds, more substantial shelters were likely constructed. These small winter sites, now abandoned for thousands of years, are extremely difficult for the archaeologist to find. We know the northern Algonkian speaking hunters, who followed a way of life not unlike the Laurentian people, frequently located their winter camps on the headwaters of streams, where they would be washed away in the spring floods.

The Laurentian peoples' belief in a life after death can be inferred from their methods of treating the dead. Objects were placed in the grave for the deceased's use in the afterlife, and bright red ochre was frequently scattered over the body. As time went on, the burial cult required greater numbers of stone, bone, and native copper implements to be deposited with the dead. Bodies were generally placed on their backs, although cremation and burial of the body in a flexed position were also practised. Adult males received most of the grave goods, suggesting that hunters were regarded with great respect in Laurentian society. Dogs were also buried, usually with adult males.

**Colour Plate I. Prehistoric Trade Items** Evidence of prehistoric trade is found in the form of exotic materials recovered from sites that are far removed from the known quarry sources of the materials in question. These trade items usually consist of an indestructable substance such as stone and copper, although it is probably safe to assume that perishable objects, such as furs, fabrics and food were also widely traded. The small white arrowhead on the upper left was manufactured from Ramah quartzite. The source of this distinctive quartzite is in northern Labrador, yet the arrowhead was recovered from a site on the Richelieu River more than 1500 air kilometres away. Below the arrowhead is a small knife from a site on the upper St. Lawrence River, which was manufactured from jasper that originated in southeastern Pennsylvania. Below the knife is a point fragment, 8000 to 9000 years old, from the same general area as the knife. It appears to be made from flint obtained from a quarry on the Gaspé coast. In the centre is a lance manufactured from Lake Superior copper and found at a 5000-year-old site on the Ottawa River. On the upper right is a knife from a St. Lawrence valley site made from a distinctive mottled flint found in New York State and southwestern Ontario.

The objects rest upon a bed of sand stained with red ochre, a material that was commonly placed with the dead, as were many of the trade items. In this way, the deceased were honoured and valuable trade goods were removed from circulation, thereby maintaining the need for trade.

**Colour Plate II. Plano Projectile Points** These points illustrate the carefully controlled stone-chipping technique that is characteristic of Plano culture. They were recovered from islands in Lake St. Francis on the upper St. Lawrence River. Such specimens have not been accurately dated in the east, but it is estimated that they are at least 8000 years old, possibly older. In this early period the St. Lawrence valley, between approximately its juncture with the Ottawa River and Quebec City was a large body of fresh water called Lampsilis Lake. Farther upstream, where these projectile points were recovered, the water levels would have been similar to those at present. Looking for sites along the present banks below the juncture of the Ottawa and St. Lawrence rivers would be useless, because this land was submerged beneath the surface of the ancient lake. Instead, the elevated beachlines of Lampsilis Lake would have to be examined. This is an example of why archaeologists must work closely with geologists when searching for evidence of early man.

Much of the information on the Laurentian culture in Quebec comes from material brought to the surface by the farmer's plough. A comparison of these objects with those excavated at sites in Ontario and New York suggests that Laurentian people in all three areas led a similar way of life. But far more specific information has been provided by excavations of two major Laurentian encampments located on islands in the Ottawa River. Both sites were fishing stations and include cemeteries. Located less than two kilometres apart, they appear to represent different times in the development of a single population. The earlier site has been radiocarbon-dated at approximately 3300 B.C. and the later site at 2750 B.C.

By comparing the two encampments, the archaeologists were able to trace changes in tool styles, burial practices, and so on, through time. Stone tools were represented by projectile points, ground-slate knives, gouges, abraders, and miscellaneous items. Atlatl weights, knives and scrapers appeared only on the earlier site, and adzes, plummets and drills were restricted to the later site. Because the limestone on the sites neutralized the acid soils, bone objects were preserved. Bone tools consisted of barbed harpoons, needles (some with eyes), awls, gorges for fishing, gouges for woodworking, projectile points, and knives made from beaver teeth. A single fish-hook, a flute made from a bird bone and a number of bone objects decorated with fine engraving were also recovered from the later site. One of the outstanding characteristics of both sites was the abundance of native copper tools: projectile points, axes, gorges, fish-hooks, awls, punches, needles (only those from the later site possessed eyes), pendants, knives and beads. Copper bracelets were found on the upper and lower arms of some of the bodies buried at the later site. Metallurgical tests indicate that the copper had been heated (annealed) to assist in the process of manufacturing the tools and ornaments.

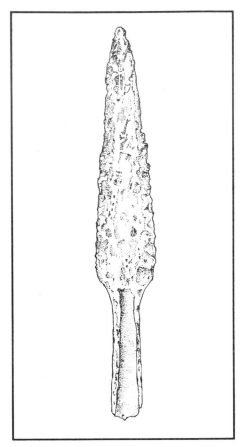

**Figure 4.** Laurentian open-socketed dart head made of native copper.

Because the nearest native copper deposits were located in the Lake Superior region, it is reasonable to assume that the Laurentian population of the Ottawa Valley had a trading relationship with the Shield populations to the northwest. The abundance of copper flakes and scraps at both sites suggests that nuggets, and not finished objects, were traded and subsequently fashioned into tools and ornaments. As in all trading relationships, there must have been reciprocity. A Shield site on Lake Temiscaming at the headwaters of the Ottawa River has produced characteristic Laurentian tools and an abundance of Onondaga flint, which probably originated in New York State. It is likely that the majority of native copper tools found on Laurentian sites in eastern Ontario, New York and Vermont, as well as in southern Quebec, were manufactured in the Ottawa Valley from copper nuggets obtained by trade from the Lake Superior region. Man's desire for exotic goods is ancient and pervasive, and led to the establishment of effective and far-ranging trade networks. These trading patterns are reflected in many of the Laurentian grave goods: conch shell pendants from the Gulf of Mexico; shell beads from the Atlantic coast; copper tools from Lake Superior; galena, a lead sulphide, from the headwaters of the Mississippi River; and rare flints from distant sources. Such objects were brought to southern Quebec by many successive hand-to-hand transactions rather than by single trading parties travelling great distances across North America.

## Shield Culture

Most of Quebec was occupied by the Shield culture during the Archaic period. During the historic period, this enormous northern region had the lowest population density per square kilometre of any region in North America. No other area of eastern Canada has such deep snow accumulations; indeed, it was from the highlands of Quebec and Labrador that the last continental

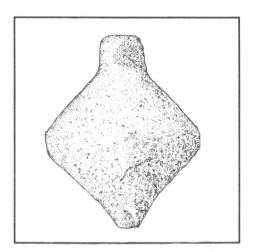

**Figure 5. Laurentian Plummet.** Often regarded as sinkers or bolas stones, these objects might also be pendants.

glacier expanded to cover most of Canada and large sections of the northeastern United States. Even today, snow sometimes survives the summer and adds to the snow build-up of the next winter, a condition that, if prolonged, could contribute to another glacial advance.

Such an environment is hostile not only to man but also to much of the game on which his survival depends. There are fewer caribou in central Quebec, for example, than in areas of the Canadian Shield farther west. Man, as a predator, must be in balance with his prey, and the small size of the population in Quebec was probably related to the limited food resources.

The Shield culture appears to have developed out of the Plano culture to the west of Quebec during the Palaeo-Indian period. As the continental glacier retreated towards the highlands of Quebec and Labrador, first plants and then animals, including predators such as man, reoccupied the land released by the ice. During this process, humans occupied the Quebec part of the Shield later than they occupied the lands to the west. Probably much of central Quebec was uninviting to man as late as 5000 years ago. This may explain why most of the Shield Archaic sites in the province, except for some in its western portion, appear to be relatively late in the Shield cultural development.

Other than stone tools and fire-fractured rock, little has survived the acid soils of the North. However, we can be fairly certain of the diet of the Shield culture. Many sites are located at the narrows of lakes and rivers which are natural caribou crossings. In addition to caribou, fish would have been an important part of the diet; in fact, this combination has probably always been necessary for survival throughout much of the desolate Shield country. The black spruce forests and their lichens, which the caribou depended upon, were frequently destroyed by fire and replaced by poplars and other plants eaten by moose. In some circumstances, the moose, rather than the caribou, would probably have been the most important big game resource, until the

**Plate 5. Dart Head and Knife** The dart head (broken) on the left and the knife on the right are typical tools of the transitional phase between the Archaic and Woodland periods in extreme southern Quebec.

black spruce forests once again reclaimed the area. Bear, beaver, hare, ptarmigan and waterfowl would also have been hunted as supplementary or seasonal resources.

The concentration of site locations on the shores of major rivers and interior lakes, as well as on islands, indicates that watercraft were used (likely birchbark canoes). Knowledge of the snowshoe must have existed because hunters would not have been able to traverse the heavy snows of winter without this ingenious device. The Shield people probably followed a way of life very similar to that of the northern Algonkian-speaking peoples of the historic period. In fact, it has been suggested that they were the ancestors of the Cree, Ojibwa, Algonkin and Montagnais.

The Shield peoples apparently did have contact with some of their neighbours. In the western part of the province a distinctive flint from northern New York State is frequently found on Shield sites. This material presumably arrived at its northern location as a result of trade with the Laurentian peoples, a proposal that is supported by the presence of characteristic Laurentian tools on neighbouring Shield sites. Such tenuous evidence of a trading network is, of course, an incomplete indication of the kind and amount of goods exchanged. We know from historic records, for example, that the Huron traded corn and nettle-fibre fish nets to the adjacent Algonkin in exchange for fish and furs. Unfortunately, such objects either do not survive in the archaeological record or cannot be definitely identified as trade items. Farther to the east there is evidence that both Shield and Maritime peoples occupied the Lake St. John area, and they possibly came into contact. Although the more northerly Shield bands would have had Palaeo-Eskimo peoples to the west and north of them, there is no evidence of their having been in contact. The Palaeo-Eskimos exploited the maritime resources of the coast, whereas the Shield peoples were mainly adapted to the interior. Probably there were large buffers of unoccupied land between the two groups, and on the basis of historical documents, we suspect that when a meeting did take place it was rarely of a friendly nature.

## Maritime Culture

The Maritime culture appears to have occupied the north shore of the St. Lawrence River and Gulf, as well as coastal Labrador and Newfoundland, for a very long time. The archaeological evidence suggests that these people entered the region nearly 9000 years ago. Their descendants have been traced for at least 6000 years, and tentative evidence suggests that an Algonkian-speaking group of the historic period were their descendants. The Maritime culture appears to have originated from the earlier Clovis culture of the Palaeo-Indian period, and current evidence indicates that only a little more than a thousand years separate late Clovis dates from the earliest Maritime dates. Unfortunately, most of the early Clovis sites along the coastal regions of the New England States, the Maritime Provinces, and the island of Newfoundland have been destroyed by the encroaching sea. Evidence suggests that the Maritime culture concentrated on coastal resources, with the result that most of their campsites on those shores have also been destroyed by the sea. Fortunately, the coastline of the north shore of the Gulf of St. Lawrence and Labrador has been rising and the early sites have been preserved. There the earliest campsites are found on the highest, hence the oldest, beach lines.

Although burial mounds constructed by the Maritime people have been found in Quebec near the Labrador border, the acid soils of the area destroyed all bone. This situation probably prevails throughout the lower north shore region of the St. Lawrence River and Gulf. However, we are able to glean some information on the burial practices and appearance of these people from a cemetery that was excavated in Port au Choix, Newfoundland. The skeletal remains from this site show that the people had a robust build. They suffered from accidental fractures, arthritis, and tooth loss caused by gum disease. Child mortality was high.

a

b

c

d

**Plate 6. Shield Stone Artifacts**

**a.** Chipped-stone dart heads.
**b.** Simple cutting and scraping tools.
**c.** Scrapers.
**d.** Large stone knives, used for scraping and graving, in addition to cutting.

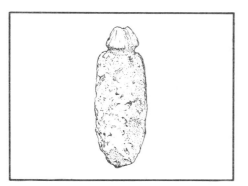

**Figure 6.** Maritime plummet manufactured from soapstone.

Elaborate grave offerings were frequently placed in the graves, particularly those of adult males. They consisted mainly of lances, daggers, harpoons and other hunting gear, although ornaments such as combs and beads and utilitarian objects such as eyed bone needles, woodworking adzes and axes have been excavated as well. A large breed of dog was also found buried with the dead. Parts from other animals, including the extinct great awk, and exotic stones, such as amethyst and quartz crystals, may have served a variety of magico-religious functions.

There is evidence that the burial ground in Port au Choix was used by the same people for over a thousand years. Many of the bodies had been buried in a highly decomposed state, which suggests that relatives kept the remains of kinsmen who had died elsewhere, possibly over the winter, for reburial in this preferred location. If a similar cemetery were to be found in the predominantly acid soils of the north shore of the St. Lawrence, an excavation would yield little more than a few grave goods manufactured from stone and some of the red ochre that was frequently sprinkled over the bodies.

One of the most unexpected aspects of Maritime culture is the erection of low burial mounds constructed of cobbles and sand. Such structures have been reported only from the extreme northeastern part of the Gulf of St. Lawrence area in both Quebec and Labrador. No bone survived the acid soil conditions in the Quebec mounds, but a similar mound, found a few kilometres to the east in Labrador and dated at approximately 5500 B.C., produced a twelve-year-old child buried face down and accompanied by abundant grave goods. Included were stone projectile points and knives, graphite paintstones for pigment, bone projectile points, a whistle, a pendant, an antler pestle, an elaborately engraved toggle, and the earliest known toggle harpoon in the world. The evidence suggests that for at least 6500 years elaborate mounds such as this were erected along this part of the Gulf. If the Labrador discovery is typical, mounds were erected over

**Plate 7. Maritime Stone Artifacts**

**a.** Typical chipped-stone dart heads of the period between 7000 and 5000 years ago.

**b.** The two stone dart heads on the left are characteristic of the period between 3500 and 4500 years ago. Associated with them are the three point-like objects on the right, which likely functioned as hafted knife-scrapers.

**c.** These crude stone cutting-and-scraping tools are found on the highest beaches along the eastern part of the Gulf of St. Lawrence. They are probably among the earliest Maritime artifacts.

**d.** Hafted knife-scraper.

**e.** Soapstone plummet.

**f.** On the left is an early style of dart head or lance, and on the right is a ground-slate dart head or lance.

**g.** Maritime woodworking gouges were similar to this Laurentian gouge.

**h.** Chipped-stone knives.

*Note:* Many of the chipped-stone tools in this photograph were manufactured from translucent quartzite found in northern Labrador, and so had to be coated for photographic purposes, thereby obliterating colour distinctions.

single rather than mass burials. Some unknown religious cult must have existed that motivated the enormous physical labour involved in the construction of such a feature over a single body — erecting mounds was obviously not the standard method used for disposing of the dead.

The discarded food bones that have been preserved because of charring, the hunting implements, and the site locations of the Maritime peoples clearly indicate that they were seafarers of considerable skill. No evidence of their watercraft has survived, but this is not surprising since the boats would have been constructed of perishable materials. Sites located on offshore islands, including the island of Newfoundland, clearly reflect the ability of these people to navigate the dangerous waters in the Gulf of St. Lawrence and along the Labrador coast almost as far as its northernmost tip.

The few food bones recovered from the campsites indicate that seal, walrus, caribou, migratory waterfowl and possibly small whales were taken. Bear and smaller mammals, such as beaver and otter, were also likely hunted. A chance stranded whale could have made a substantial, if irregular, contribution to the food supply. Fish remains do not preserve well, but it is inconceivable that the Maritime people were not capable of exploiting the rich salmon, cod and capelin resources of the area. The fixed and toggling harpoon heads and points, possibly from specialized fish spears, all indicate the exploitation of marine animals. Some food resources that could well have been crucial for existence simply do not survive in the archaeological record. The massive schools of capelin that spawn in the summer, for example, require no more specialized tool than the hands to capture; they are easily preserved by drying and are consumed whole. Some site locations along sandy beaches may have been chosen specifically to exploit this small fish during its short spawning period. Similarly, the St. Lawrence River eel fishery, so important to the natives during the historic period, would leave little or no record in the archaeological deposits.

**Plate 8. Restored Maritime Burial Mound** Found at L'Anse-Amour in southern Labrador. An adolescent burial accompanied by abundant grave offerings was discovered below the central cist. Dated at 7500 years, it is the oldest-known burial mound in North America. Similar mounds in adjacent Quebec are likely as old.

In order to survive by hunting and fishing, man had to possess an intimate knowledge of the seasonal behaviour of the animals that he depended upon for food. The more alternatives he had, the better were his chances for survival. For example, if the capelin arrived late, it was necessary to have seabird nesting areas or grey seals nearby, or an emergency cache of dried seal or caribou meat. Although subject to local variations, the seasonal rounds probably consisted of seal hunting from late winter to early summer; salmon and capelin fishing, egg gathering and bird hunting in the summer; and caribou hunting in the interior in autumn and early winter.

The role the caribou played in the seasonal rounds of the Maritime adaptation is still speculative. Caribou range as far as the coast in summer but only small amounts of their bones have been found at coastal sites. They were more numerous in the fall

**Plate 9. Central Cist of a Maritime Burial Mound** View of the central stone cist of a Maritime burial mound near Blanc Sablon on the north shore of the Gulf of St. Lawrence. The cist, made of stone slabs set vertically in the ground, was restored after the mound under which it lay had been excavated.

and early winter in the interior. Yet the only definite evidence of Maritime campsites in the interior has been found on Lac de la Hutte Sauvage on the George River in northeastern Quebec. This site's tools, frequently made from the Ramah quartzite of Labrador, appear late in the tradition and date about 2000 B.C. Studies have suggested that, before 5000 years ago, much of the highland interior of Quebec and Labrador would have been of little use to either man or caribou because of the aftermath of deglaciation and the nature of the plant communities (alder and birch thickets) that occupied the freed land. Perhaps small bands of Woodland caribou wintered closer to the coast during its early occupation by man.

About 2000 B.C., deteriorating climatic conditions made the occupation of much of the eastern Labrador coast untenable for Maritime hunters. Shortly after their disappearance, Palaeo-

**Colour Plate III. An Archaeological Surprise** In 1966, during a road excavation at Sillery, Quebec, workmen destroyed an ancient grave. The body is reported to have been liberally sprinkled with red ochre and was accompanied by abundant grave offerings. Fortunately, a number of the artifacts were made available for study and these were assigned to the Adena culture. The heartland of Adena culture is in the Ohio Valley, nearly 1300 kilometres to the southwest, and so the discovery was a surprise to archaeologists. Recently, however, an Adena burial mound dated at 380 B.C. was excavated in northeastern New Brunswick. It now appears that elements of the Adena burial cult were adopted by the indigenous people of the Northeast, or possibly that actual Adena immigrants were involved. The large knives and points are actually 3 cm longer than in the photograph. Such specimens are characteristic of Adena culture, and are frequently manufactured from exotic stone. Even more typical is the tubular pipe, at the bottom, that was manufactured from a distinctive stone whose source is in Ohio.

Eskimo hunters appeared from the north to take their place. What happened to the former occupants? Proof is still lacking, but it appears that they moved south to join their kinsmen on the island of Newfoundland and along the Quebec and Labrador shores of the Gulf of St. Lawrence. One piece of evidence leads to this conclusion. Near the north end of Labrador is found the distinctive Ramah quartzite. This high-quality, glass-like stone (a silica) was not only well suited for the manufacture of stone tools, but may also have been aesthetically valued for its translucence. It was widely traded in prehistoric times and has been found on sites as far south as Maine and Fort Lennox on the Richelieu River in southern Quebec. Late Maritime sites along the north shore of the Gulf of St. Lawrence characteristically contain an abundance of this material.

The Maritime culture in the St. Lawrence estuary presents one of the greatest challenges to archaeologists working in Quebec. A framework is slowly emerging, but the extent of the area involved and its apparent time span of nearly 6000 years ensure years of research before we can even begin to understand many aspects of this cultural development. For example, what were the relationships between the Maritime and Laurentian peoples? We know that they might have been in contact in the Tros-Rivières area, that they shared a number of common tool varieties and burial practices, and we are told by the physical anthropologists that they appear to have been closely related. What were the relationships between the Maritime and Shield peoples? Shield peoples occasionally travelled as far as the coastal regions to exploit its rich resources and might have come in contact with Maritime peoples. Who occupied most of the Gaspé Peninsula — the Maritime culture, the Shield culture, a local group that evolved from the earlier Plano occupation, or elements of all three cultures? Did the descendants of the Maritime culture become some of the eastern Algonkian-speaking peoples of the historic period? Only further research will provide the answers.

**Plate 10. Maritime Stone Artifacts from a Quarry Site near Tadoussac**
**a.** Bit end of a gouge.
**b.** Dart heads.
**c.** Ground-stone adze.
**d.** Flaked celt with a ground bit.
**e.** Scraper.
**f.** Ground-slate rod of uncertain use.
**g.** Range of knives, some of which were probably hafted.

**Colour Plate IV. Polished Stone Tools** While most prehistoric stone tools in Quebec were chipped into shape, some were ground and polished using abrasive material such as sandstone.   The objects in this picture came from the Ottawa Valley. On the left is a large slate object whose use may have been ceremonial. At the bottom, centre, is a Laurentian Archaic slate atlatl weight (see Fig. 3). In the lower right hand corner, is a rare object called a "boatstone." The latter item, whose function is unknown, is more characteristic of the Adena and Hopewell cultures to the south; indeed, the implement appears to have been manufactured from a distinctive Ohio stone. On the upper right is a slate pendant with drilled suspension hole that probably was manufactured by a Point Peninsula craftsman.

# CHAPTER 3

# The Woodland Period
## (1000 B.C. – the Historic Period)

The Woodland period begins with the first appearance of pottery vessels. Evidence now exists to show that the preceding Laurentian peoples and some of the other Archaic cultures adopted pottery and were thereby transformed into Woodland peoples. No major changes took place in cultural development other than the introduction of this single item of material culture. Pottery sherds, which are readily recognizable, practically indestructible and often abundant, provide the archaeologist with a convenient device for dividing prehistoric time into more manageable units.

As is shown on Map 5, not all the Archaic peoples of Quebec adopted pottery vessels to the same extent. In the extreme western part of the Canadian Shield, the upper St. Lawrence valley, and the Eastern Townships, these vessels are common features. But along the coast of the lower St. Lawrence River and Gulf they are not as prevalent, and many of the later sites in this region are devoid of pottery. This irregular pattern of pottery adoption in Quebec has created certain classification problems for the archaeologist that do not exist in Ontario, the Maritime Provinces, and the adjacent American states, where pottery was accepted by everyone, or in Newfoundland, where it was never adopted (except for rare occurrences along the Labrador coast). The Shield peoples of the extreme western part of Quebec, for example, adopted pottery, whereas their kinsmen throughout the rest of the province rejected this new item. Thus the classificatory association of the term *Woodland* and the introduction of pottery is only partially applicable in Quebec. In the descriptions of the Woodland cultures that follow, mention will be made of contemporaneous groups that did not use pottery.

The Woodland period has been divided into the Initial Woodland period and the Terminal Woodland period. The first period encompasses those Archaic peoples who adopted pottery between 1000 B.C. and 500 B.C. and their descendants to approximately A.D. 1000. The second period refers to the prehistoric cultures that can be traced to historic populations, such as the St.

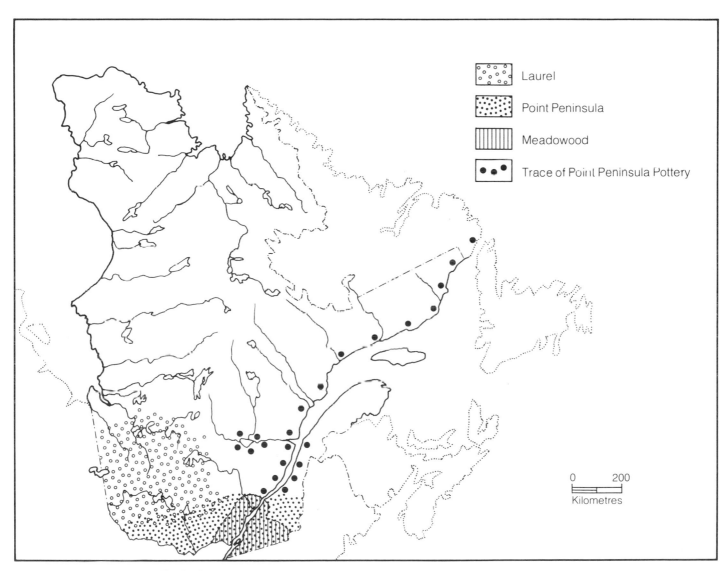

**Map 5. Initial Woodland Period**

Legend:
- Laurel
- Point Peninsula
- Meadowood
- Trace of Point Peninsula Pottery

0 200 Kilometres

Lawrence Iroquois (Hochelagans and Stadaconans) and the Montagnais. It should be emphasized that the dividing line of A.D. 1000 between the Initial and Terminal Woodland periods is an artificial device whose sole purpose is to divide prehistoric time into more manageable units. At some future date, when archaeological research has provided more information, this clumsy device may be replaced by outlines of the various developing cultural traditions.

## The Initial Woodland Period

The independent invention of pottery has occurred a number of times in the New and the Old Worlds. An early form of pottery that appeared in the upper St. Lawrence River valley and Eastern Townships around 1000 B.C. consists of simple straight-sided vessels with pointed bottoms. Both the inner and outer surfaces of most of these containers were impressed with a cord-wrapped object while the clay was moist prior to firing; however, some have smooth sides or impressions on only one surface. The knowledge of pottery appears to have spread northwards from the southeastern United States, where it had existed as early as 2000 B.C. When the Archaic people in southern and eastern New York, Pennsylvania and Massachusetts learned to make pottery, they began producing pottery vessels that were identical to their earlier soapstone vessels. The beaker-shaped, cord-impressed and plain containers came into use later and were introduced to the late Laurentian peoples in southern Quebec, adjacent New York State, and parts of southern Ontario. These people are known as the Meadowood culture.

### Meadowood Culture

Most of our knowledge of the Meadowood culture comes from burials excavated in Quebec, New York and Vermont. The burial practices of the late Archaic period were continued and embellished. Cremation became more popular and the deceased were generally provided with an abundance of stone and copper goods. Earlier tools such as the gouge, the spear-thrower or atlatl weight, and the ground-slate knife and lance were replaced by the mysterious birdstone ( a highly stylized, ground-slate bird form whose function is unknown), the ground-slate gorget and other new items. There is some tentative evidence to suggest that another new object of technology, the bow and arrow, made its appearance at this time and that it gradually took the place of the older atlatl- or throwing board-propelled javelin or dart. In addition to tools, the graves contain carefully flaked, triangular flint blades, which were apparently made specifically for burial with the dead. Natural minerals such as ochre, limonite and graphite, possibly used for painting the body and other objects, frequently appear in the graves, as does powdered red ochre.

Nothing can be said about the physical appearance of these people, because their remains have been destroyed by cremation or acid soils. It may be assumed, however, that they resembled their Laurentian ancestors and suffered from the same sorts of ailments.

One of the rare, known campsites of the Meadowood people, located near Trols-Rivières, contains hearths. A badly wind-eroded cemetery was also found behind the site on a higher terrace. A small amount of bone and shell from the habitation site has survived and has been identified as black bear, moose, beaver, turtle, and freshwater clam. Beaver, turtle and clam remains were the most abundant.

Projectile points, similar in form to those of the late Laurentian culture, and numerous scrapers were found. Other items included knives, drills, graphite nodules, abraders, and native copper chisels, awls and a fish-hook. Many of the stone tools were manufactured from a distinctive mottled flint found in New York State and adjacent southwestern Ontario. Other varieties of stone came from the Eastern Townships or farther south, and the

a

b

c

d

e

f

g

h

i

**Plate 11. Meadowood Artifacts**
**a.** Typical dart heads.
**b.** Native copper implements: on the left, a tubular bead; below centre, an object of unknown function; and on the upper right, a fish-hook.
**c.** Birdstone. Such objects probably had a religious function, as they are most frequently found in graves.
**d.** Rim fragment from a pottery vessel decorated with cord impressions.
**e.** Large stone knives fragmented by fire. Grave offerings were sometimes placed in the crematorium.
**f.** Scrapers.
**g.** Knives.
**h.** Graphite nodule used as a paintstone.
**i.** Drill.

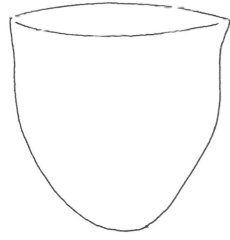

**j.** Outline of a Meadowood pottery vessel.

native copper probably came from the Lake Superior region. We know from other sites that Meadowood people maintained wide-ranging trade connections, a fact that is reflected in the stone and copper materials found on their sites.

The evidence suggests that the Meadowood people followed a way of life similar to that of their Laurentian ancestors. The appearance of pottery in the Laurentian culture (of the Archaic period) caused archaeologists to rename it the Meadowood culture (of the Initial Woodland period). Similarly, the adoption of a new variety of pottery ushered in a new culture – the Point Peninsula. Its presence was first indicated by a single pottery sherd found at the Meadowood site near Trois-Rivières. Shortly thereafter new pottery styles replaced the earlier forms and archaeologists created yet another name for the same people. This may be confusing, but it must be remembered that archaeologists deal with the few cultural remains that survive the passage of time. Therefore, when one variety of pottery is replaced by a quite different style, it provides another convenient device for refining the limited control archaeologists have over prehistoric developments in both time and space.

## Point Peninsula Culture

Although widely distributed throughout the upper St. Lawrence River valley, the lower Ottawa River valley, and the Eastern Townships, few Point Peninsula sites have been excavated. Like most Archaic sites, the later Point Peninsula sites are small, many of them representing seasonal encampments at favourable fishing locations. Where significant changes in water levels have not taken place, the Point Peninsula materials are frequently found mixed with the earlier Laurentian refuse.

In contrast to the somewhat simple, straight-walled, cord-impressed vessels of the Meadowood culture, the Point Peninsula pottery includes some of the best examples of the potter's art to be found in the province. Early Point Peninsula vessels have

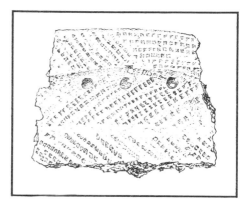

**Figure 7.** Rim fragment from a Point Peninsula pottery vessel, decorated with a toothed instrument.

**Plate 12. Point Peninsula Artifacts**
**a.** Rim fragments from typical pottery vessels.
**b.** Stone abrader, probably used for sharpening celts, shaping bone tools, and other similar functions.
**c.** Stone effigy platform-pipe.
**d.** Ground-slate pendant with a drilled hole for suspension.
**e.** Stone darts or arrowheads.
**f.** Bone harpoon head.
**g.** Stone drills.
**h.** Scrapers.
**i.** Bear canine tooth with hole drilled through the root for suspension.

pointed bases. They were decorated by impressing, rocking, or dragging toothed implements on the wet clay to form a wide range of designs. With time, the vessels became larger and the bases more rounded. Collars were added and new decorating techniques, such as impressing the clay with a stick wrapped with cord, increased in popularity.

Just as the pottery styles changed through time, so did the stone tools, represented mainly by projectile points and scrapers. Polished stone axes, ground-slate pendants with one hole, abraders and other minor tool types are present. Evidence of fishing equipment is scarce, even at sites where discarded fish bones are found. Stone net-sinkers and bone fish-hooks, gorges and harpoons are present, but in limited numbers. A braided basket was a rare discovery at one site. It had been accidentally preserved by being burnt and then buried.

The earliest Point Peninsula ceramics from Quebec are almost identical to those from southern Ontario, northern New York and Vermont, and from as far away as the Maritime Provinces. The limited scattering of Initial Woodland pottery found along the north shore of the St. Lawrence River and Gulf belongs to the earliest styles. The similarity in decorative design and vessel form suggests that when the new pottery was introduced into Quebec it spread very rapidly. Throughout most of the province, however, pottery was either not accepted or was adopted half-heartedly. After its minimal acceptance by inhabitants of the North Shore, it was apparently abandoned, and does not reappear until the Terminal Woodland period. In the upper St. Lawrence, the lower Ottawa valley, and the Eastern Townships, pottery became a firmly entrenched element of the material culture. Here, as time went on, certain varieties of pottery became identified with specific regions, whereas stone and bone tools generally remained similar over a much larger area. Perhaps the plastic nature of pottery permitted a greater degree of individual expression despite the ever-present requirements of cultural conformity.

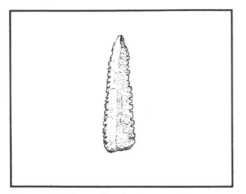

**Figure 8.** A toothed, stone pottery-decorator used for making impressions similar to those on the rim fragment in Figure 7.

While these regional ceramic varieties were evolving, another significant cultural item was introduced from the south — smoking pipes. The appearance of these rare pipes carved from soapstone, however, does not necessarily mean that tobacco was grown. Even relatively late in the historic period, the Indians of eastern North America smoked a wide range of plants for a wide range of purposes. For example, hawthorn bark was smoked with other elements to attract deer during the hunt, and wooly yarrow was smoked during certain ceremonies.

By about A.D. 800, a number of the regional expressions of the Point Peninsula culture had begun developing into those of the Terminal Woodland period. In southeastern Ontario, one development led to the historic Huron and Petun Iroquoian cultures. In northern New York, the Mohawk, Onondaga and Oneida cultures materialized, and in the upper St. Lawrence valley in Quebec, a third regional expression developed into the historic St. Lawrence Iroquois — the Hochelagans and the Stadaconans. (It was the St. Lawrence Iroquois that Jacques Cartier encountered in the early sixteenth century and that disappeared from the area by 1603, when Samuel de Champlain began his explorations.) All of these Terminal Woodland developments terminated in Iroquoian-speaking peoples. Indeed, it would appear that the Point Peninsula culture, like its predecessor, the Laurentian culture, consists mainly of populations that spoke a variety of Iroquoian dialects.

Adjacent groups, probably speaking some form of the Algonkian language, also shared Point Peninsula pottery styles to varying degrees. Along the Ottawa River, for example, the Point Peninsula culture follows roughly the same development that led to the historic Huron and Petun in Ontario. In this instance, the end product appears to have been various bands of the historic Algonkin.

In making these observations, archaeologists have not underestimated the danger of inferring language from broken bits of

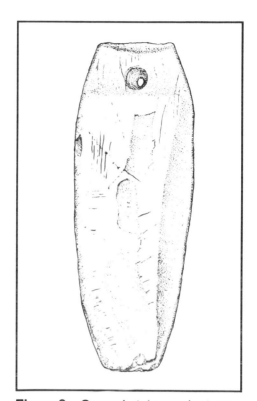

**Figure 9.** Ground-slate pendant, perforated for suspension.

pottery and other tools. The information that is available, however, indicates a continuity in the prehistoric record over many thousands of years. It is unlikely that an intruding foreign population would displace the indigenous populations without seriously disrupting the continuity that is reflected in the archaeological material culture. Such a displacement did take place in the Eskimo prehistory of the province, and the dramatic cultural discontinuity caused by it has been clearly preserved in the archaeological record. With few exceptions, however, the evidence from prehistory of one population over-running another pertains to farmers and pastoralists, people who possess some control over their food supply. Because there were no pastoralists in North America and the time period under consideration precedes the introduction of corn farming, the case for cultural continuity appears to be better founded than the case for major cultural displacement.

## Laurel Culture

The Laurel culture occupied all of northern Ontario, most of Manitoba, and east-central Saskatchewan. In the extreme west of Quebec it is represented by bands of Shield Archaic hunters who adopted pottery. Their kinsmen to the east did not use pottery and continue to be classified as Shield people into the historic period.

Although the knowledge of pottery must have been introduced from the south, the Shield people in western Quebec did not adopt southern pottery styles. Instead, they learned the skills needed to manufacture the new item and developed their own pottery complex. Early Point Peninsula pottery had similar origins. In fact, Laurel and Point Peninsula ceramics share a number of common traits. Vessels from both cultures are characteristically wide-mouthed with pointed bases. Decoration is restricted to the upper portions of the Laurel vessels, the lower parts being carefully smoothed. Cord impressions were rarely or never used; most

**Figure 10.** Unfinished stone platform-pipe, above, and outline of pottery vessel, below.

**Plate 13. Laurel Artifacts**
**a.** Rim fragments from typical pottery vessels.
**b.** Hammerstone.
**c.** Stone knife.
**d.** Knife made from a beaver incisor.
**e.** Toggling harpoon head made of antler. Such harpoons were likely used for capturing large fish such as sturgeon.
**f.** Net-sinker made of a flat rock notched at both ends.
**g.** Native copper arrowheads.
**h.** The various designs in the plasticine (left) were made by means of the stone pottery-decorator (right).
**i.** Copper chisel.
**j.** Copper needle.
**k.** Copper beads.
**l.** Stone arrowheads.
**m.** Scrapers.
**n.** Lance head.
*Note:* The artifacts in this illustration came from northern Ontario. Adequate specimens for illustration from Quebec were not available in the collections of the National Museum of Man.

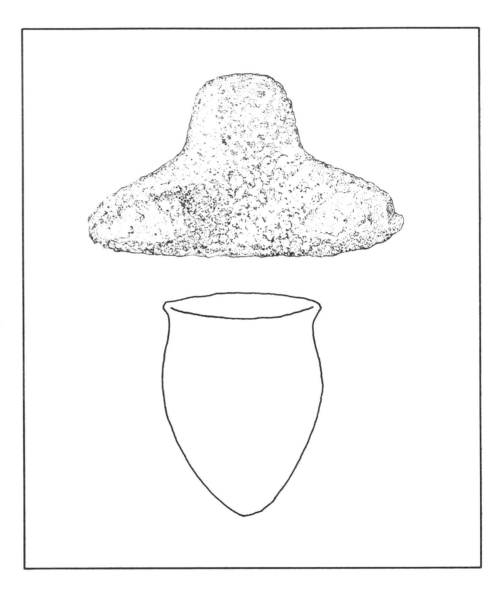

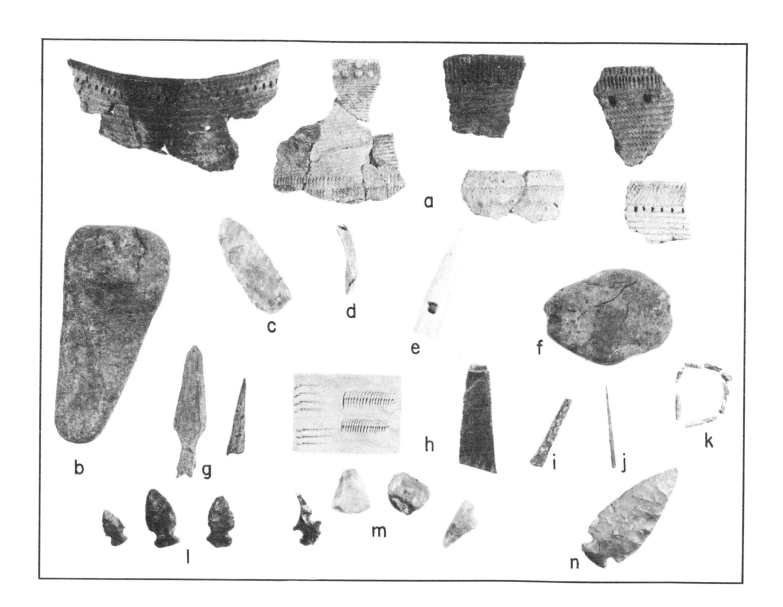

of the designs were executed with toothed implements that were impressed into the clay.

The Laurel people followed a way of life unchanged from that of their Archaic predecessors and their non-pottery-using kinsmen to the east. Most of the Laurel sites are on lakes or along river-lake systems, generally at good fishing locations. They were probably summer campsites where families of the local band gathered when and where there was sufficient food for all. With the coming of winter, however, the individual families would be forced to return to their separate hunting grounds. The limited winter resources of a small area could not support larger groups. Unfortunately discovering these small winter campsites in the dense Boreal Forest of the Shield is very difficult.

No bone tools have been recovered from Laurel sites in Quebec because of the acid soil conditions that prevail in the area. Stone tools are those typical of late Shield sites: scrapers, projectile points, knives and hammerstones. (Scrapers are the most abundant.) Nothing, of course, remains of the wooden, bark and leather goods, such as canoes, snowshoes, lodges, and toboggans, that must have been the most common and elaborate items of their material culture. The Laurel people in Quebec and adjacent eastern Ontario were apparently in close contact with the Point Peninsula people to the south. Such items as polished stone axes and exotic southern flints are common on Laurel sites, presumably as a result of a trading relationship.

## The Terminal Woodland Period

Two language groups are involved in the Terminal Woodland period in Quebec: the Iroquoian, represented by the St. Lawrence Iroquois, and the Algonkian, represented by the Cree, Algonkin, Montagnais, and the Micmac-Malecite. The cultures of the Terminal Woodland period developed directly from Initial

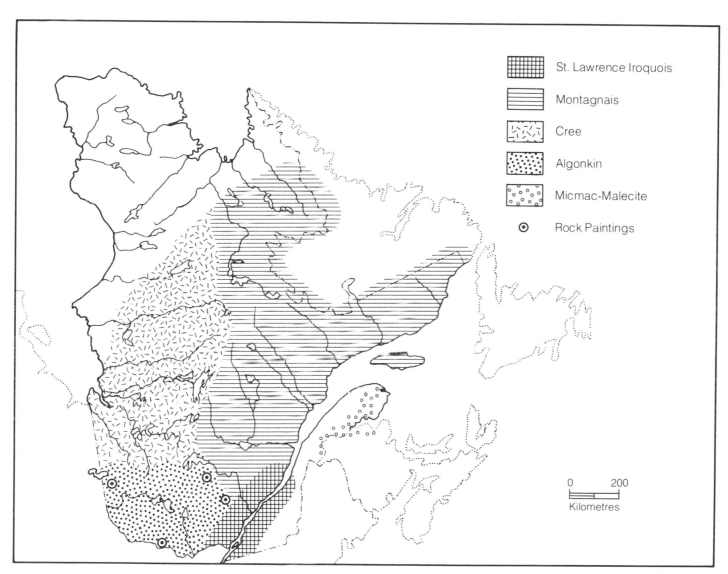

Legend:
- St. Lawrence Iroquois
- Montagnais
- Cree
- Algonkin
- Micmac-Malecite
- Rock Paintings

0    200
Kilometres

**Map 6. Terminal Woodland Period**

Woodland period cultures and from cultures that did not accept pottery, thus retaining their archaeological classification of Archaic.

## The St. Lawrence Iroquois

In the early sixteenth century, Jacques Cartier visited villages occupied by Iroquoian-speaking peoples, who lived in the region extending from Quebec City upriver to Montreal. There were actually two populations in this area: the Stadaconans downriver and the Hochelagans upriver. A boundary located just upstream from Trois-Rivières separated the two groups. Both the Hochelagans and Stadaconans lived in semipermanent villages. They grew corn, beans and squash, and supplemented their diet with fish and game. The Stadaconans, however, occupied an area in which corn growing was marginal and they were forced to rely more heavily upon hunting and fishing, thus following a way of life that was somewhat similar to their Algonkian-speaking neighbours'. When Samuel de Champlain visited the same area in 1603, it was abandoned. An alliance of Montagnais, Algonkin and Huron was locked in war over its ownership with the League of Five Nations Iroquois, who lived in northern New York State.

Who were the St. Lawrence Iroquois, where did they come from and what happened to them between the Cartier and Champlain visits? Much has been written in an attempt to answer these questions, but before describing the archaeological evidence, it is useful to examine the historical information on these people.

The Stadaconans were the first Iroquoian people encountered by Jacques Cartier. During his explorations of the Gulf of St. Lawrence and the northeastern coast of the Gaspé, he met a fishing party from the village of Stadacona at Gaspé Bay and took two of the natives back to France. A small glossary of Stadaconan words was collected at this time and was later identified as Iroquoian by some of our first linguists. Modern methods of linguistic analysis have only recently determined that the Stadaco-

**Figure 11.** St. Lawrence Iroquois clay trumpet-pipe.

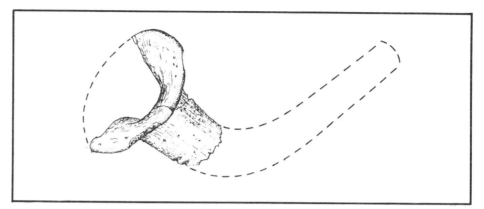

nan language was a distinct Iroquoian language rather than a Huron or Mohawk derivative, as was originally believed.

Cartier's reports mention six Stadaconan villages, all on the north side of the St. Lawrence River: Stadacona (now Quebec City); Ajoaste, Starnatan, Tailla, and Sitadin a short distance downstream; and Achelacy upstream. The French explorers do not appear to have been impressed with these villages, indicating that they were probably small. Cartier mentions that they were not protected by palisades.

Fortunately for us, Jacques Cartier recorded his one-day visit to the village of Hochelaga (now Montreal). He also mentioned that there were two other villages in the general area whose people spoke the same (similar?) language as the Stadaconans. Cartier's description of the village is interesting:

*The village is circular and is completely enclosed by a wooden palisade in three tiers like a pyramid. The top one is built crosswise, the middle one perpendicular and the lowest one of strips of wood placed lengthwise. The whole is well joined and lashed after their manner, and is some two lances in height. There is only one gate and entrance to this village, and that can be barred up. Over this gate and in many places about the enclosure are species of galleries with ladders for mounting to them, which*

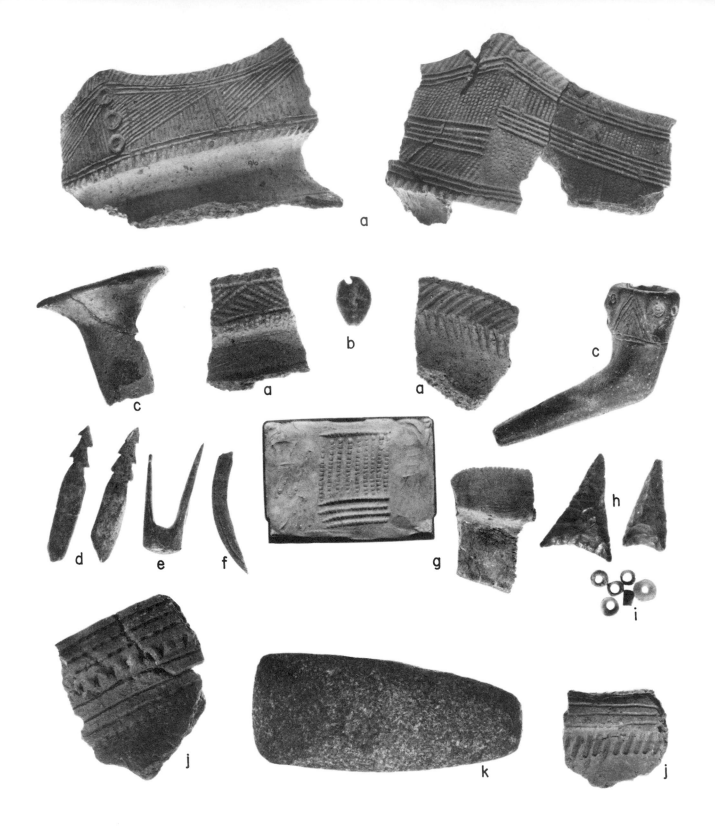

a

c                    a                    b                    a                    c

d                    e                    f                    g                    h

i

j                    k                    j

**Plate 14. St. Lawrence Iroquois Artifacts**

**a.** Rim fragments from typical pottery vessels.

**b.** Stone effigy of a human face, probably an amulet.

**c.** Typical ceramic smoking pipes.

**d.** Bone arrowheads.

**e.** Bone fish-hook.

**f.** Beaver-incisor knife.

**g.** Impressions in the plasticine (left) were made with the notched turtle-shell pottery-decorator (right).

**h.** Stone arrowheads.

**i.** Stone beads.

**j.** Rims from pottery vessels made between A.D. 1200 and A.D. 1300.

**k.** Polished stone adze.

*galleries are provided with rocks and stones for the defence and protection of the place. There are some fifty houses in this village, each about fifty or more paces in length and twelve or fifteen in width, built completely of wood and covered in and bordered up with large pieces of the bark and rind of trees, as broad as a table, which are well and cunningly lashed after their manner. And inside these houses are many rooms and chambers; and in the middle is a large space without a floor, where they light their fire and live together in common. Afterwards the men retire to the above-mentioned quarters with their wives and children. And furthermore there are lofts in the upper part of their houses, where they store the corn of which they make their bread.* *

These observations parallel seventeenth-century European descriptions of Huron, Petun, Neutral, Mohawk, Onondaga, Oneida, Cayuga, Seneca and Susquehannock villages, suggesting that the Hochelagans followed a similar way of life. Archaeological excavations have confirmed and enlarged upon these descriptions.

The relations between the Hochelagans and the Stadaconans are interesting. Cartier mentions that the Hochelagans ruled all of the tribes farther downstream, which presumably meant the Stadaconans. On the other hand, the Stadaconans attempted to stop Cartier from advancing upsteam to Hochelagan country. This might have been an attempt by the Stadaconans to maintain for themselves the most favourable trading position with the French. By cutting off their Hochelagan kinsmen from direct trade, they might have hoped to establish themselves in the profitable position of middlemen.

The Hochelagans referred to a tribe that wore wooden-slat armour and lived up the Ottawa River as *agojuda,* or "evil men."

---

*H.P. Biggar, *The Voyages of Jacques Cartier,* Publications of the Public Archives of Canada, no. 11 (Ottawa: King's Printer, 1924), pp. 155-57.

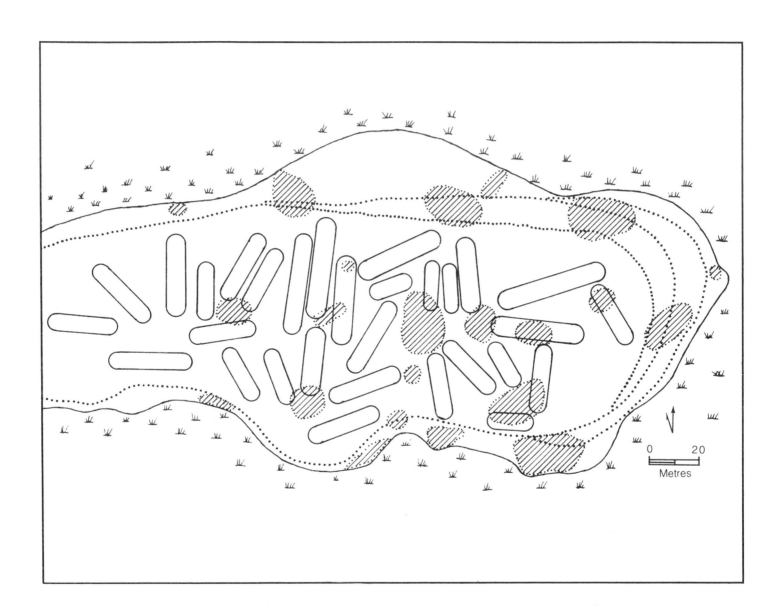

**Figure 12. Simplified Floor Plan of a St. Lawrence Iroquois Village** This floor plan of a St. Lawrence Iroquois village is derived from archaeological evidence, and is more typical than the engraving done by Gian Baptista Ramusio in 1556 (see Figure 13). This village could have contained as many as forty longhouses, ranging from 18 to 41 metres long and accommodating more than 2000 people. Whereas many aspects of Cartier's description compare closely with those of later European observers of Iroquois villages, Ramusio's engraving of Hochelaga is not only schematic but highly inaccurate in many details. It almost certainly represents the artist's conception based upon Cartier's verbal description.

As the route up the Ottawa River leads to Huronia and as we know the Iroquoian tribes used slat armour until the introduction of the musket, these "evil men" were likely the Huron. The Stadaconans, on the other hand, were in constant conflict with their neighbours, the Toudamans, who were likely the Micmac and the Malecites. However, they appear to have been on good terms with the adjacent Montagnais. They were also friendly with a tribe to the west from whom they obtained copper. Because the nearest native copper sources are located at the east end of Lake Superior, these peoples were probably Algonkins.

Archaeological research is only now beginning to establish the origins of the St. Lawrence Iroquois. It appears that they evolved from a late Point Peninsula culture in the upper St. Lawrence River valley in Quebec and Ontario. About A.D. 1000, corn agriculture was introduced from southeastern Ontario or northern New York, where as early as A.D. 800 corn-growing people had been living in longhouses in stockaded villages. The effective integration of agriculture into the St. Lawrence Iroquois subsistence pattern caused a population explosion that overflowed the heartland between Lake St. Francis and Lake St. Louis on the St. Lawrence, spilling into Ontario and New York upstream and to Trois-Rivières downstream. The major shift appears to have been into Ontario and adjacent northern New York State. About A.D. 1400, some of the St. Lawrence Iroquois groups probably expanded farther downstream to become the ancestors of the historic Stadaconans.

The main St. Lawrence Iroquois villages were located some distance from the major waterways, probably for defensive reasons. They were sometimes surrounded by multiple stockades, and one site could have contained as many as forty longhouses, ranging in length from 18 to 41 metres, with an average length of 30 metres. As many as 2000 people could have lived in one of these villages. In addition to the main villages, there were small fishing hamlets along the shores of the St. Lawrence River in both Quebec and Ontario.

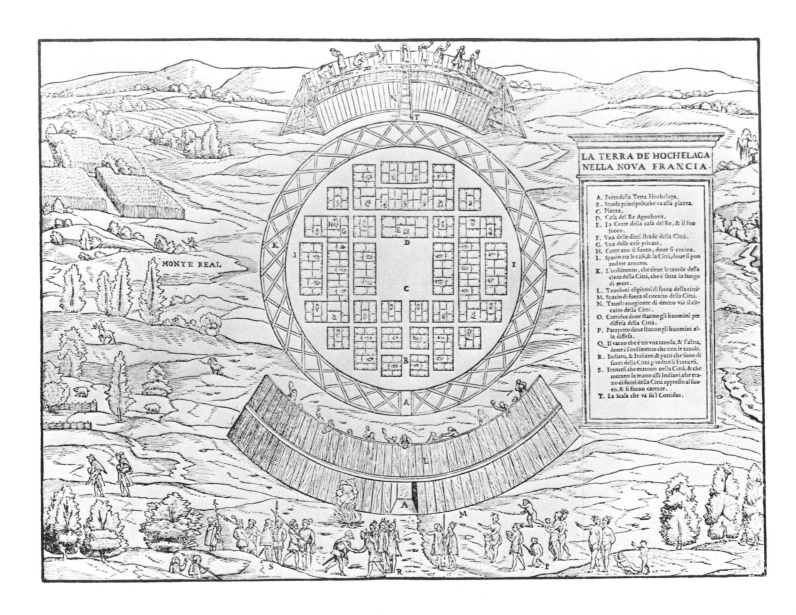

LA TERRA DE HOCHELAGA
NELLA NOVA FRANCIA.

MONTE REAL

A. Porta della Terra Hochelaga.
B. Strada principale, che va alla piazza.
C. Piazza.
D. Casa del Re Agouhanna.
E. 1a Corte della casa del Re, & il suo
   fuoco.
F. Vna delle dieci strade della Città.
G. Vna delle case priuate.
H. Corte con il fuoco, doue si cucina.
I. Spacio tra le case, & la Città, doue si puo
   andare attorno.
K. L'ordimento, che tiene le tauole della
   cinta della Città, che e fatta in luogo
   di mure.
L. Tauoloni cógionti di fuora della città.
M. Spacio di fuora al circuito della Città.
N. Tauole congionte di dentro via il cir-
   cuito della Città.
O. Corridor doue stanno gli huomini per
   diffesa della Città.
P. Parapetto doue stanno gli huomini al-
   la diffesa.
Q. Il vacuo che è tra vna tauola, & l'altra,
   doue è l'ordimento che tien le tauole.
R. Indiani, & Indiane, & putti che sono di
   fuori della Città p vedere li Francesi.
S. Francesi che entrono nella Città, & che
   toccano la mano alli Indiani, che era-
   no di fuori della Città appresso al fuoco, & si fanno carezze.
T. La Scala che va su'l Corridor.

70

**Figure 13.** Gian Baptista Ramusio's illustration of the village of Hochelaga. Reprinted from H. P. Biggar, *The Voyages of Jacques Cartier,* Publications of the Public Archives, no. 11 (Ottawa: King's Printer, 1924), pl. 9.

The St. Lawrence Iroquois buried their dead within the village, often in the house floor. From the excavated skeletal material, we know that they suffered considerable tooth decay, probably because of their high-carbohydrate diet of corn. (In addition to corn, the garbage dumps contain beans, squash, and sunflower seeds.) Other conditions, such as arthritis, were also common, and the infant death rate was high. Physical anthropology indicates that the St. Lawrence Iroquois belonged to the Iroquoian physical type.

The pottery art of the St. Lawrence Iroquois, in both vessel shape and artistic design, equalled, if not surpassed, that of all other Iroquoian groups. They used bone to a far greater extent in making various implements than their neighbours did, possibly because flint suitable for tool manufacture was scarce in their area. There is abundant evidence of charred and broken human bones, as well as ornaments and tools made from parts of the human skeleton. When it is possible to identify the sex and age of these human remains, they are found to belong to adult males. This coincides with the evidence found in historical documents indicating that the various Iroquoian tribes tortured and ate enemy warriors and adopted the women and children not killed in battle.

What happened to the St. Lawrence Iroquois who vanished sometime between the voyages of Cartier in 1535 and Champlain in 1603? There is archaeological evidence that most of the St. Lawrence Iroquois were absorbed by the Huron. This seems to have happened while an eastern branch of the Huron occupied the Trent River drainage basin in eastern Ontario, shortly before they moved northwest into Huronia, at the foot of Georgian Bay. It has been mentioned that historic Iroquoians killed enemy warriors but adopted the women and children. Reports by the early explorers and missionaries indicate that Iroquoian women tended the corn, bean and squash crops and manufactured the pottery vessels, and Iroquoian men tended the tobacco fields

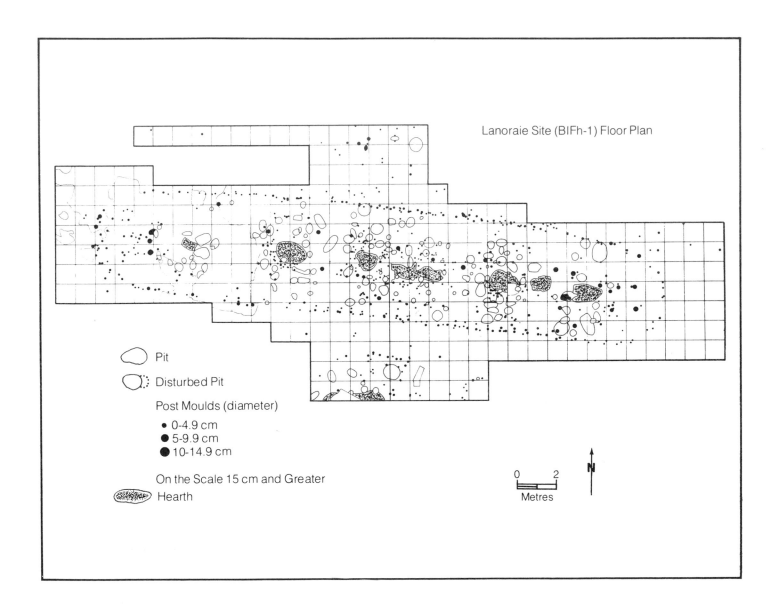

Lanoraie Site (BIFh-1) Floor Plan

Pit

Disturbed Pit

Post Moulds (diameter)
- 0-4.9 cm
- 5-9.9 cm
- 10-14.9 cm

On the Scale 15 cm and Greater
Hearth

0    2
Metres

N

**Figure 14. Floor Plan of a St. Lawrence Iroquois Longhouse**
This house, located in a prehistoric village site to the southwest of Trois-Rivières, would date prior to 1500. It is 29 metres long and nearly 6 metres wide. Down the central corridor there appear to be five hearth-and-pit concentrations. If two families shared a hearth, as was the case during the historic period, then ten families might have lived in the house. A section of another house can be seen to the south of the completely exposed structure. The floor plan illustrates how the archaeologist records the stains left by posts, pits and hearths dug into the house floor by the original inhabitants. Location and size of posts are indicated by the black dots, and the hearth remnants by stippling.
(Courtesy of Georges Barré, Service d'archéologie et d'ethnologie, Québec.)

and made the smoking pipes. Huron sites contemporaneous with the disappearance of the St. Lawrence Iroquois contain a high percentage of the characteristic St. Lawrence Iroquois pottery but little or no evidence of the equally distinctive St. Lawrence Iroquois pipes. This suggests that the influx of St. Lawrence Iroquois peoples into the eastern Huron villages was not a voluntary move; otherwise, all items of their material culture, including the pipes, the characteristic bone arrowheads, and other tools, would be present in the excavations. In addition, the small quantities of Huron pottery and cannibalized remains recorded from the western St. Lawrence Iroquois sites suggest that a state of war had existed between the Huron and the St. Lawrence Iroquois for some time. No St. Lawrence Iroquois ceramics have been found in the villages of their other potential enemies, such as the Onondaga and Oneida in nearby New York State. It appears, then, that the *agojuda*, or "evil men," that the Hochelagans told Jacques Cartier about referred to the Huron.

The destruction of the St. Lawrence Iroquois is puzzling. The social need for warriors to acquire prestige hardly called for such drastic action. One possible explanation is economic. Just as the Stadaconans attempted to stand between French trade and the Hochelagans, so the Hochelagans attempted to control European trade into the interior. We now know that a trickle of European trade goods was reaching the present Toronto area by 1500 – before Cartier's first voyage. These materials likely came from Europeans fishing in the Gulf of St. Lawrence, who unfortunately did not record their activities for posterity. This trade apparently had had a dramatic impact upon the native populations of the St. Lawrence and lower Great Lakes regions, long before anyone in the interior saw a European. It is probable that the Huron, Algonkin and Montagnais alliance that was locked in battle with the Iroquois League of Five Nations over possession of the St. Lawrence River, and thereby the European trade, was the same alliance responsible for the destruction of the St. Lawrence

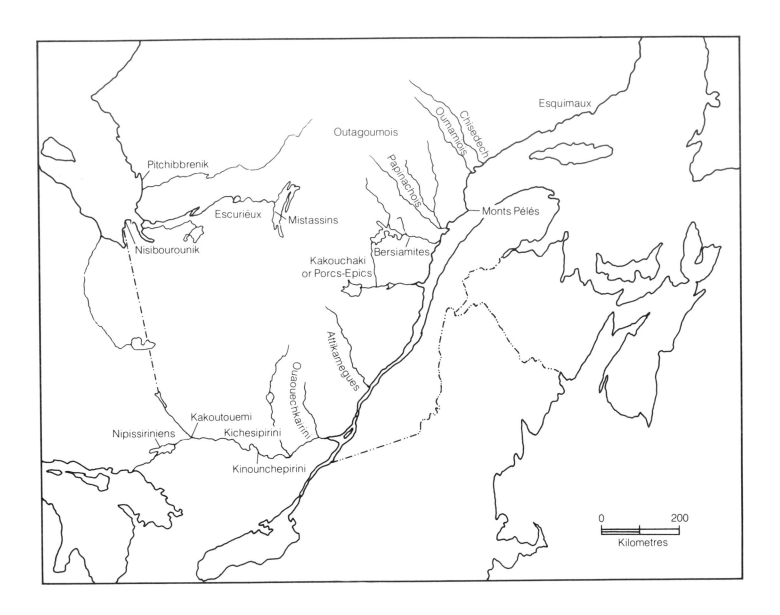

Esquimaux

Outagoumois

Ounamois

Chisedech

Pitchibbrenik

Papinachois

Escuriéux

Mistassins

Monts Pélés

Nisibourounik

Bersiamites

Kakouchaki
or Porcs-Epics

Attikamegues

Ouaouechkairini

Kakoutouemi

Nipissiriniens

Kichesipirini

Kinounchepirini

0          200
Kilometres

74

**Map 7. Location of Algonkian-speaking Bands During the First Half of the Seventeenth Century.** Based on a map from Roger Marois, *Les schemes d'établissement à la fin de la préhistoire et au debut de la periode historique: le sud du Québec.* Collection Mercure, Commission archeologique du Canada, 17 (Ottawa: Museum of Man, 1974).

Iroquois. In the mid-seventeenth century it was the Huron's turn; they were dispersed, absorbed or destroyed by the Iroquois League of Five Nations for the same reason that the St. Lawrence Iroquois were destroyed — control of the European trade.

## The Algonkin

From a language and cultural standpoint, the Algonkin are related to the Cree and Montagnais. All three populations were composed of small, independent and highly mobile bands. However, sufficient differences exist to tell them apart. The term *Algonkin* is used to link a number of related but independent bands that share closer blood and cultural ties with one another than they do with their related neighbours. The terms *Cree* and *Montagnais* are used in the same way. Families could, and did, move from one band to another, and intermarriages among members of the three major groups were probably common. In Champlain's early-seventeenth-century records, for example, the Algoumequins, the Allumette Islanders, the Quescharini or Petite Nation, and the Quenongebin, all located on the Quebec watershed of the Ottawa River, and the Iroquet, located between the Ottawa and St. Lawrence rivers, are classified as Algonkins, as are related groups in adjacent Ontario.

With only a few exceptions, the stone tools of the Algonkin, Cree and Montagnais appear quite similar. There are some cultural elements, however, that distinguish the three groups. For example, the small number of rock paintings in southwestern Quebec were likely painted by Algonkins and represent the eastern extremity of a cultural practice that extended across northern Ontario, Manitoba and Saskatchewan. The painting of these religious records, executed in red paint on sheer rock faces, was common to the Ojibwa and Cree to the west. The sedentary St. Lawrence Iroquois and Huron-Petun villagers also exerted considerable cultural influence upon the adjacent Algonkins. They shared a ceramic complex with Huron and Petun to the west, from as early as A.D. 800 in some areas. Most of the Algonkin bands grew corn during the historic period, and there is evidence that corn was also grown in prehistoric times. Historical records indicate that Algonkin groups and families even wintered in Huron villages. This relationship appears to have been quite old, and was likely based on a reciprocal trading pattern. In historic times, this trade involved the exchange of Huron corn and fish nets for Algonkin furs and meat. The Shield ancestors of the Algonkin had been exposed to similar southern influences from the Laurentian culture and later from the Point Peninsula culture.

The Algonkin's sharing of Huron-Petun ceramics has created problems for the archaeologist. When fragments of this pottery are found, it is difficult to know whether they are Algonkin or Huron. I suspect that Huron trading or warring parties did not carry cumbersome and fragile pottery vessels on their travels. On excavated sites in Quebec, these sherds are found with the distinctive Algonkin stone tools.

Many Algonkin sites also contain a small amount of pottery that is not of Huron or Petun origin. This pottery relates to Ojibwa and other western Algonkian-speaking peoples, indicating that intermarriage took place among the various Algonkian groups. Algonkin women were far more mobile than men. Their duties of rearing children and tending fish nets did not require them to have an intimate knowledge of the local area and the cooperation of kinsmen as did the male duty of hunting. One result of this mobility was that women established family links that stimulated trade and contact among distant bands. This pattern also extended to the east, where Huron-like pottery has been found on Montagnais sites on Lake St. John and the Saguenay River. Does this pottery indicate that Algonkin women married Montagnais men, or that Algonkin bands had moved into Montagnais territory? The first explanation seems to be the more likely.

Huron-Petun pipe styles are also found on Algonkin sites. It is impossible at present to distinguish between Huron pipes traded to the Algonkin and Algonkin pipes manufactured in the same style as the Huron. The problems that this situation presents can be seen at the St. Lawrence Iroquois site in Montreal. It was long thought to be the village of Hochelaga (Tutonaguy) but is now believed to be a near-contemporaneous sister village. This site yielded a small quantity of Huron pottery and pipes, which has been regarded as evidence of the presence of Hurons on the site; however, it may be that these remains belonged to visiting Algonkins using Huron-like pottery and pipes.

The stone tools used by the Algonkin, which are very different from those of adjacent Iroquoian groups, consist of many small stone scrapers, knives, and a range of unnotched and notched triangular shaped arrowheads. The latter are fashioned with little modification of the original flake — an atypical Iroquoian trait. In the relatively rare instances where bone has survived the usually acid soils, items such as awls, beaver-tooth chisels, and unilaterally barbed harpoons are found. Dog burials are common on Algonkin sites.

During the turbulent latter half of the seventeenth century, when the Huron, Petun and Neutral of Ontario, and other Iroquoian- and Algonkian-speaking populations were dispersed or absorbed by the League of the Iroquois, the Algonkin retreated to the northernmost extremities of their territory and to the mission posts. Many shifted westward with the fur trade and joined other Algonkian-speaking people. As the conflict subsided, some of the Algonkin bands reoccupied their old territories and reside there to this day.

**The Cree**
Like the Algonkin, the Cree consisted of a number of independent bands of hunters and fishermen. In late prehistoric times, this

a

b

c

d

e

f

g

h

i

j

**Plate 15. Algonkin Artifacts**

**a.** Rim fragments from pottery vessels; the three specimens on the left belong to a ceramic tradition that was shared with the Huron and Petun, whereas the two specimens on the right belong to a completely different tradition.

**b.** Stone arrowheads.

**c.** Soapstone smoking pipe.

**d.** Scrapers.

**e.** Chipped-stone celt, ground at the bit end.

**f.** Beaver-incisor knife or chisel.

**g.** Stone knife.

**h.** Stone knife.

**i.** Notched stone, possibly a net-sinker.

**j.** Knife manufactured from native copper that originated in the Lake Superior area.

large grouping of bands occupied most of northern Saskatchewan and Manitoba as well as northwestern Ontario. Since the Ojibwa and Algonkin appear to have occupied all of central and northeastern Ontario, how and when did a group of Cree establish themselves in the northwestern portion of Quebec? It has been suggested that they moved east with the fur trade; however, there is some archaeological evidence from lakes Mistassini and Albanel of a local Shield cultural development that terminated in the present Cree population. The Cree, Montagnais, Ojibwa and Algonkin languages are closely related; Cree being closest to Montagnais, and Algonkin closest to Ojibwa. One archaeological hypothesis suggests that all of these people developed out of the Shield culture but in regionally different ways. The Cree to the west of Quebec, for example, possessed a distinctive ceramic complex that included, in some areas, plates and bowls as well as pots. The Cree of Quebec, on the other hand, did not adopt ceramics, and, if the archaeological reconstruction is correct, they retained a very old form of Shield culture tool manufacture. Hopefully, further work in this little-known area will resolve these problems.

French records for the first half of the seventeenth century report four groups that are now regarded as Cree: the Mistassins in the Mistassini Lake area, the Escurieux along the Rupert River, the Nisibourounik to the west of the mouths of the Nottaway and Rupert rivers on James Bay, and the Pitchibarenik near the mouth of the Eastmain River. Probably other bands were located to the north of these.

Of future interest to archaeologists are the historic locations of the Nisibourounik and Pitchibarenik on James Bay. Do their locations indicate that a substantial part of their subsistence was drawn from the sea? What was their relationship to the nearby Inuit communities to the north? Archaeological rescue operations conducted during the development of the James Bay hydroelectric project may provide some of the answers to these questions.

**Colour Plate V. St. Lawrence Iroquois Pottery Vessel** The St. Lawrence Iroquois potter surpassed all other Iroquois peoples in the skill and artistry with which she fashioned her cooking vessels. Clay would be carefully cleaned, grit added, and the vessel then shaped by hand. The decoration was done by incising or impressing the wet clay with a variety of tools. After drying in the sun, the pot would be fired upside-down over an open hearth. The peaked elevations (called castellations), sometimes found along the lip, were ornamental rather than functional. Vessels such as this were used to cook the corn gruel that was a basic part of the diet of all Iroquoian peoples. Archaeologists often find thick layers of carbonized food adhering to the inside of such pots, suggesting that inattentive cooks can be found in all societies.

The manner in which pottery vessels were formed and decorated was dictated by cultural values that changed through time and differed from one area to another. Therefore, pottery fragments are very useful to the archaeologist in his effort to define sequences of cultures and to trace their geographical distribution.

Caribou, moose and fish were likely the Cree's major sources of food, because corn and other domesticated plants could not be grown in the area. In such a harsh land, all possible food resources had to be exploited. The timely appearance of migrating waterfowl could well have tipped the balance between starvation and survival after the winter food supply had been exhausted, and even today the arrival of geese and ducks in the spring is awaited with keen anticipation.

The Cree appear to have been relatively isolated. Their recorded locations in the first half of the seventeenth century remained basically unchanged during the latter half of the same century. In contrast, during this last period, the Algonkin to the south had been dispersed as a result of their conflict with the League of the Iroquois. This, of course, does not mean that the Cree bands lived in a vacuum. It is historical knowledge that the Kakouchaki (Porcupine), a Montagnais group who occupied the Lake St. John area, acted as middlemen for the interior bands with regard to the trade coming out of Tadoussac. When the Cree bands travelled south to trade their pelts for European goods, they would have had the opportunity to exploit the rich fish resources of the lake, contract marriages, and participate in other social events. There is some archaeological evidence that a distinctive quartzite from the Mistassini Lake area found its way, in the form of tools and flakes, to the southeast as far as Lake St. John. This suggests that a prehistoric trading pattern existed.

The only detailed archaeological information on the Cree comes from the Mistassini-Albanel region. With the exception of some of the quarries where tools were made, the excavated sites are small and have relatively thin cultural deposits. There are a large number of these sites in the region. This is to be expected of a small population that had to range over large areas because of limited food resources. Acid soils have destroyed all bone, and only the stone tools survive. These tools are typical of the earlier Shield culture, and consist mainly of many large knives and

**Plate 16. Firestones** In order to roast meat or boil water, prehistoric man frequently used stones heated over a fire. Meat would be placed on the hot rocks, or rocks would be dropped into water to bring it to a boil. This process would cause the rocks to fracture in a fashion that is not duplicated by nature. Such mundane objects are frequently the first indication of prehistoric man that the archaeologist encounters.

Quebec and Labrador would have been essential to their survival.

From earliest times, the St. Lawrence River and Gulf has probably been a major area of friendly or hostile cultural contact. The Stadaconans, for example, told Jacques Cartier that "they descended the Great River from Chelogua in order to make war on those first seen,"* the Micmac on Chaleur Bay, and that they lost nearly 200 people in a Toudaman (Micmac and/or Malecite) attack on a temporary island campsite opposite the Saguenay River (possibly Île Verte or Île aux Basques). Similarly, Micmac legends describe wars with the Kivedech and the destruction of a group of their people by a party of "Iroquois" in the Bay of Bic. The Kivedech, or Iroquois, were almost certainly the Stadaconans. The aim of the above description is not so much to bring attention to the conflict between the Stadaconans and the Micmac-Malecite as to reflect the mobility of people living along the St. Lawrence River and Gulf. The more southerly Montagnais bands, who had ready access to the St. Lawrence, clearly show the results of being close to this major travel route. Pottery styles typical of the upper St. Lawrence and northern New York are recovered from their sites, as are exotic flints and copper traded down river.

At the beginning of the sixteenth century, when the Stadaconans and Toudamans were at war, Montagnais bands were occupying the north shore and had been since A.D. 900, and likely much earlier. French records for the first half of the seventeenth century list a number of Montagnais bands or groups: the Attikameg on the headwaters of the Rivière Saint-Maurice, the Kakouchaki around Lake St. John, the Betsiamites on the lower reaches of the Rivière Betsiamites, the Papinachois on the Rivière aux Outardes and the Rivière Manicouagan, the Monts Pélés on the coast at Pointe des Monts, the Oumamiois on the Rivière

---

*André Thevet, *Les singularitez de la France antarctique* (Paris: Maissonneuve, 1878), p. 401

Sainte-Marguerite, the Chisedech on the Rivière Moisie, the Esquimeaux (a Montagnais group rather than Inuit) along the north shore opposite Anticosti Island, and the Outagoumois in the highlands between the Eastmain River draining into James Bay and a series of rivers draining into the St. Lawrence River. All of these bands or groups were in the same locations in the second half of the seventeenth century, except the Attikameg to the west and the Esquimeaux to the east. To this day, many still occupy parts of their ancient homelands.

An important Montagnais site was recently discovered near Mingan, opposite the western end of Anticosti Island. The discovery occurred by accident. During the excavation of the late-seventeenth-century trading post of Louis Joliet, it was found that the post had been built over a Montagnais site that extended from the historic period (down through a number of layers) to approximately A.D. 900. One such site can provide archaeologists with more information than a score of single, unstratified campsites.

Small scrapers dominated the tool assemblage on the Mingan site. The arrowheads, the next most common item, were largely corner-notched triangular forms, although stemmed, simple triangular and side-notched varieties were also present. Many of these points possessed characteristics typical of the various Algonkian cultures. Triangular knives and harpoon heads were less common, as were polished stone axes and abraders. A number of the chipped-stone tools had been manufactured from Ramah quartzite from the northeastern Labrador coast. This quartzite has been found at other Montagnais sites as far away as Lake St. John. Other objects recovered from the site were stone pipe fragments and a native copper awl from one of the prehistoric strata, and European trade goods and numerous seal bones from the historic strata.

Of great interest is the small amount of pottery recovered from most strata. Aside from some crude, undecorated specimens from the upper levels of the site, most of the pottery is typical of the cultural development that led to the Mohawk, Onondaga and Oneida groups in northern New York. The vessels date from A.D. 900 to 1200. Only one vessel was decorated in a style typical of the nearer St. Lawrence Iroquois. A site at Kagashka, east of Mingan, yielded pottery similar to that made in southern Ontario about A.D. 1300, and the same kind of pottery has been recorded from Iroquoian sites farther up the St. Lawrence River. One explanation for the strange ceramic mixtures found at these eastern Montagnais sites is that Iroquoian ceramic influences spread down the Richelieu River from northern New York about 1000 years ago, and somewhat later from Ontario and southern Quebec via the St. Lawrence River. The vessels could also have been produced by captive Iroquoian women. At Montagnais sites in the Lake St. John and Chicoutimi areas, St. Lawrence Iroquois and Huron ceramics are often found together. It would appear that the Montagnais, like most of the northern Algonkian-speaking peoples, shared a number of different pottery traditions; a fact that must certainly reflect the mobility of women within their society.

On the basis of the limited evidence available, it appears that the Montagnais bands evolved from a Shield cultural base in much the same manner as their Algonkin and Cree relatives. If this is true, the question arises as to what became of the late Maritime populations along the north shore of the Gulf of the St. Lawrence. Did they develop into some of the eastern bands of the Montagnais, or were they absorbed by the ancestors of the Montagnais? Did they shift to the island of Newfoundland, where they contributed to the historic Beothuk populations? Or did they move across the Gulf of St. Lawrence into the Maritime Provinces? Only future research will answer these questions.

## The Micmac-Malecite
The Micmac and the Malecites, who still live in the Maritime Provinces, share a common culture and language. They speak

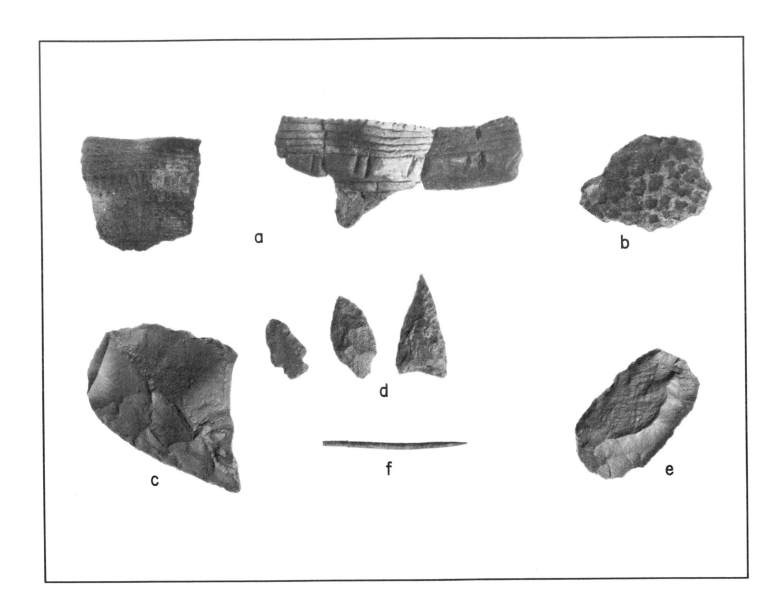

**Plate 17. Montagnais Artifacts**
**a.** Rim fragments from pottery vessels; the style of decoration of the specimen to the left is similar to pottery found in northern New York State, whereas the other rim fragment is similar to the pottery styles from southern Ontario.
**b.** Sherd from the body of a pottery vessel.
**c.** Large scraper manufactured from Ramah quartzite, a material originating in northeastern Labrador.
**d.** Arrowheads.
**e.** Scraper.
**f.** Bone awl.

Algonkian languages that are quite distinct from those spoken by the Montagnais, Cree and Algonkin.

During the summer, the Micmac-Malecite exploited the rich maritime resources of their country, and in the winter they scattered into the interior in search of big game. Their coastal sites indicate a heavy reliance on shell-fish gathering. It has been suggested that at one time they practised corn farming to a limited degree.

The prehistory of the Micmac-Malecite is still in its infancy. Nevertheless, work along the south side of Chaleur Bay in New Brunswick has yielded material that likely relates to these people and is pertinent to the prehistory of Quebec. The assemblage consists of many scraping tools; very thin and finely flaked lanceolate projectile points, as well as notched and stemmed forms; knives; a few polished axes; and a distinctive type of cord-impressed pottery. Similar materials have been recovered from a site at Cap-Chat on the north side of the Gaspé Peninsula and from sites in the Lac Témiscouata region. Radiocarbon dates for these range from A.D. 500 to 1200.

Although the major historic locations of the Micmac-Malecite were in the Maritime Provinces, these people would have had ready access to the north side of the Gaspé Peninsula along the coast or up major rivers, such as the Saint John or Matapedia, and the tributaries of the Restigouche. They appear to have been on much better terms with the Montagnais than with the Stadaconans. This is borne out by Father Le Jeune's report of his 1633 winter trip with a band of Montagnais from Tadoussac into the Témiscouata region, in which he noted that his companions were familiar with the area. Neither Jacques Cartier nor any of the other early European explorers reported seeing native villages along the south shore of the lower St. Lawrence River. It has been suggested that the region acted as a buffer zone between the warring Stadaconans and the Toudamans (Micmac-Malecite). It is hoped that further research will resolve the question of whether

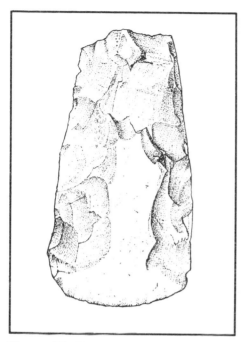

**Figure 15.** Chipped and ground celt.

**Plate 18. Micmac–Malecite Artifacts**
**a.** Large rim fragment from a typical cord-decorated pottery vessel.
**b.** Polished-stone celt fragment.
**c.** Stone knife and knife fragments.
**d.** Arrowheads.
**e.** Scrapers.

the Micmac-Malecite seasonally occupied the Gaspé coast. During the early historic period, Micmac-Malecite, Montagnais and Stadaconans all exploited the area on a seasonal basis. Possibly the Micmac-Malecite inhabited the Gaspé before the St. Lawrence Iroquois expanded down the St. Lawrence River. As a result of the Stadaconan expansion, a territorial feud which was still active in the early historic period, might have broken out between the two groups.

## The Abenaki
Even less can be said concerning the Abenaki, who lived in the Eastern Townships of Quebec. From written records, we know that part of the Abenaki confederacy lived in southeastern Quebec in large, sedentary villages surrounded by fields of corn and the other crops they cultivated. A small amount of evidence indicates that some of the historic Abenaki bands may have occupied the area in late prehistoric times, but beyond this no other comment is possible at present.

# CHAPTER 4

# Palaeo-Eskimo and Thule Cultures
## (2000 B.C. – A.D. 1450)

### Palaeo-Eskimo Culture

Nearly 4000 years ago, a people with a culture that was dramatically different from any other discussed to this point occupied the arctic coastal margins of Quebec. These people were part of a movement out of northern Alaska that constituted the first human occupation of the Canadian High Arctic and Greenland. Equipped with a sea-mammal hunting technology and capable of surviving far north of the treeline, they were the first hunters to exploit the rich food resources of the Far North. Since there was no competition from earlier hunters in the area, the Paleo-Eskimos spread rapidly throughout most of the North, including even the northernmost islands of the Arctic Archipelago. Their descendants were to occupy parts of coastal Quebec for approximately 3500 years.

According to physical anthropologists, the small quantity of Palaeo-Eskimo skeletal remains found in northern Quebec and Newfoundland belong to the Eskimo racial stock. Apparently these people, for the most part, exposed their dead to scavengers and the elements and, as a result, only a few remains have survived.

The earliest Palaeo-Eskimos spread rapidly along the coasts of Quebec and Labrador. By about 1500 B.C. they had reached as far south as Poste-de-la-Baleine, slightly north of the juncture of Hudson Bay and James Bay. By 1800 B.C. they had occupied much of the north coast and had sparsely settled the Labrador coast as far south as Hamilton Inlet.

Archeologists have given the earliest Palaeo-Eskimos regional names: Independence I, Independence II and Sarqaq in Greenland as well as in the eastern High Arctic, and Pre-Dorset in most of the Canadian Arctic. Almost all of the remains from Quebec are Pre-Dorset, although Sarqaq influences are also evident.

Early Palaeo-Eskimo sites in Quebec are always located in areas rich in seal and other sea mammals. There is only limited

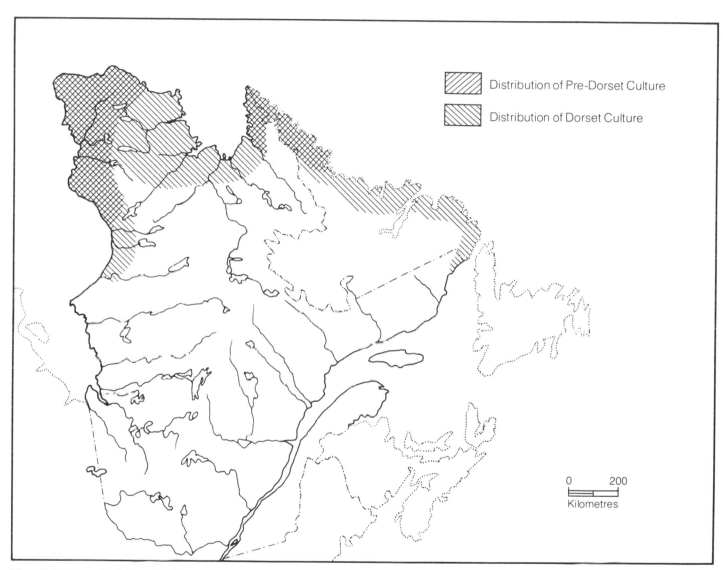

**Map 8. Palaeo-Eskimo Cultures**

Distribution of Pre-Dorset Culture

Distribution of Dorset Culture

0     200
Kilometres

**Plate 19. Dorset Structure** The people standing in the foreground are at the ends of a rectangular Dorset structure, 26 by 9 metres discovered in Ungava Bay. In the background is a stone grave-vault, indicated by the arrow.

evidence of significant exploitation of the interior caribou herds. House structures were simple, circular tent-rings ranging from 4 to 5 metres in diameter and sometimes containing recognizable central hearth floors. Occasionally the tent coverings were held down by large cobbles and at other times by heaps of gravel. These tents were presumably made of skins supported by wooden poles.

Along the eastern coast of Hudson Bay, the land was depressed by the weight of the ice during the last glaciation but is now slowly rising. This is called isostatic rebound. The average uplift along this coast is estimated at 1.2 metres per century, and, as a result, an early Palaeo-Eskimo (Pre-Dorset) site near Poste-de-la-Baleine is now approximately 69 metres above sea level. A rising coast provides a relative means of dating; the oldest sites are on the highest beaches and the most recent on the lowest beaches.

The tools used by the early Palaeo-Eskimo people (Pre-Dorset culture) were usually very small and delicately fashioned. Indeed, an earlier name for this and related cultures was the Arctic Small Tool tradition. Among the stone tools are small triangular-shaped and stemmed points for arrows and harpoon tips; sideblades that were shaped to fit into slots cut into bone lance heads to increase penetration; various scraping and cutting tools; burins, specialized stone implements for engraving, which were sharpened by striking off small flakes; and long, thin flake knives, which were struck from specially prepared cores. Often the flints from which these tools were made are of a very high quality and may have been selected for aesthetic reasons. Small chipped and ground adze blades have also been recovered.

The acid soils of northern Quebec have destroyed most of the culture's bone and ivory tools, and there is, of course, no evidence of the wooden implements that once existed. On the basis of early Palaeo-Eskimo excavations elsewhere, however, it can be suggested that toggling harpoon heads, eyed needles, needle cases, and large, open-socket lance heads were used. The coastal and island locations of sites, plus the recovery of food bones, point to a sea-mammal economy heavily oriented towards seal. Fish, birds and other mammals would also have been exploited during the seasonal rounds. It can be inferred from the site locations that some form of watercraft was used (possibly the kayak).

The late Palaeo-Eskimo Dorset culture is a direct development from the earlier Palaeo-Eskimo Pre-Dorset cultural base and seems to have evolved in the same area of the eastern Arctic, including the northern coastal region of Quebec. There do not appear to have been any major cultural changes, although certain tool types disappear and new ones appear. Indeed, the entire Palaeo-Eskimo development is characterized by conservatism. A major change that did take place was the expansion of

**Plate 20. Profile of a Dorset Site**
Profile of an early, stratified Dorset campsite showing a thick clay deposit capping the uppermost cultural layer. The collapsed portion of the wall to the right is due to melting of the permafrost.

the Dorset population. The Pre-Dorset occupation of coastal Quebec and Labrador was sparse and incomplete. On the other hand, the Dorset occupation, at least in certain areas, appears to have involved greater numbers of people. The expansion of the Dorset culture southward along the Labrador coast, and a portion of the north shore of the Gulf of St. Lawrence, into Quebec, and onto the island of Newfoundland is particularly striking. In Newfoundland, the Dorset people established themselves from about 500 B.C. to A.D. 750 along the coast of the entire island. Their appearance on the eastern coast of Hudson Bay, however, was

**Plate 21. Excavation of a Dorset Site**
Test excavations have just begun on this late Dorset site. The two depressions in the foreground are the remains of 600-to-700-year-old Dorset semisubterranean houses.

later (circa A.D. 800), and although the population appears to have declined, it did survive into the fifteenth century. On the north coast the entire span of the Dorset culture, beginning with its transition from Pre-Dorset to its disappearance in the fifteenth century, is represented. What caused this expansion? What was the reason for the two thousand year gap between the appearances of the Pre-Dorset and Dorset peoples along the eastern coast of Hudson Bay? Climatic changes recorded on the northern coast do not offer any clues. Prior to 850 B.C. the climate was warm, between 850 B.C. and A.D. 350 it was cold, between 350

**Colour Plate VII. Weapon Tips from Lake Abitibi** Since it is often difficult for an archaeologist to know if a weapon tip was hand-thrusted into an animal or was propelled by a throwing board or a bow, these implements are collectively called projectile points. Projectile points, more so than many other implements, are characteristic of certain prehistoric cultures and time periods and are, therefore, very useful to the archaeologists in establishing chronologies and relationships. These projectile points all come from a single site on Lake Abitibi in western Quebec. The broken point at the bottom could be as old as 4000 to 5000 years. From left to right along each of the three rows from the bottom up, the point styles become progressively later until the historic period is reached with the point in the upper right corner that was manufactured from a piece of a European brass kettle. Obviously the site was used for many thousands of years by different bands of hunters.

and 1280 it was warm again, and from 1250 on it was cold again. Did changing ocean currents modify pack-ice conditions and, therefore, the availability of seal and walrus? One factor or, more likely, several factors must have made conditions of life more agreeable in the south, particularly along the eastern coast.

The Dorset sites in Quebec are situated in locations similar to those of their Pre-Dorset ancestors. Along the eastern coast of Hudson Bay, where isostatic rebound is taking place, the Dorset sites are located on the lower strandlines, and the Pre-Dorset sites are situated on the higher, more ancient beaches.

Dorset houses in Quebec tend to be larger than the earlier Pre-Dorset houses, suggesting that they were two-family or extended-family dwellings. Along the eastern coast of Hudson Bay, the houses are clustered in small groups of from two to five structures. One summer house, 6 metres in diameter, has a slightly depressed floor, half of which is paved with flat rock slabs. The unpaved portion was probably the sleeping area. A poorly defined hearth floor and a rock-lined pit are also present. Another house in the same area, regarded as a winter dwelling, because of its more substantial nature, was obviously constructed for two families. It measures 4.5 metres in diameter and has a shallow excavated floor and an earth ring around the perimeter for holding down the tent flap. A carefully laid pavement of flagstones occupies the central area of the structure, and carefully made hearths occur at either end. A single storage pit is recorded.

The structures excavated in Newfoundland are quite different from these houses. Newfoundland winter houses are square to rectangular in outline, are semisubterranean with built-up stone walls, and have a line of stone-faced pits running down the centre of the floor from front to back. Raised, semicircular sleeping platforms are found at the rear of the houses. Deep storage pits are also present. Presumably, if Dorset houses were to be discovered along the north shore of the Gulf of St. Lawrence in Quebec, they would resemble the Newfoundland structures.

**Colour Plate VIII. Palaeo-Eskimo Artifacts** Most of these artifacts come from Palaeo-Eskimo sites in the Ungava region of northern Quebec, although a few are from sites along the north shore of the Gulf of St. Lawrence. With the exception of the two flaked burins in the far-right middle of the photograph, all of the specimens belong to the late Palaeo-Eskimo Dorset culture. These two exceptions are characteristic tools of the early Palaeo-Eskimo Pre-Dorset culture.

On the upper left are toggling harpoon heads made from bone, antler or ivory. The three on the far left did not require stone tips, whereas the two on the right have inset stone points, one of which is illustrated. Below the harpoon heads are three miniature harpoons and a small point, which may have been used as hunting charms. Below these are three eyed needles of bone and a small bird-dart.

In the centre of the photograph is a small ivory mask, which bears a close resemblance to the etched face on the cover of the book. Below the mask is a delicate carving of a polar bear. On either side of the carvings are bone lances; the one on the left is missing an end piercing-point but has a stone side-blade in place; the one on the right has a ground-slate piercing point, with the side blade removed from its slot. (Side blades would enlarge the wound and increase the bleeding.)

On the upper right are a number of chipped- and ground-stone harpoon tips. Below these are five ribbon-like flint blades or microblades, which are characteristic of all Palaeo-Eskimo cultures. Below the two Pre-Dorset burins are two ground-stone Dorset burins. In the lower right-hand corner are a row of scrapers. Directly below the carvings and lances is an ice-creeper; these would be lashed to the feet to permit the hunter to move over smooth ice without slipping. To its left is a miniature ladle, and beside it is an artifact that is either a bone awl or a projectile point.

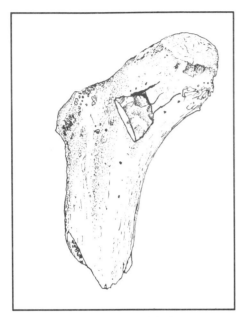

**Figure 16.** Walrus rib with the imbedded tip of a Dorset stone point.

In northern Quebec and along the eastern coast of Hudson Bay, late Dorset longhouses have been recorded. These structures vary in size, with some measuring more than 30 metres in length. Only the stone elements have survived from these multiple-family dwellings, which must have been covered by skins supported on wooden poles.

Most of the Dorset tools clearly reflect their Pre-Dorset origins. Toggling harpoon heads, lances with stone tips and sideblades, scrapers, blades struck from prepared cores, and various knives all have Pre-Dorset equivalents. However, new items, such as soapstone cooking vessels, ground burins, and whalebone sled shoes do appear. A small breed of dog is now known from Dorset sites. The abundant food bones found on many sites indicate that the Dorset people were sea-mammal hunters, particularly of seal and walrus. Caribou, fox, birds, polar bears, and beluga whales were also taken.

One of the outstanding aspects of Dorset culture is its art. Small ivory and bone carvings of animal and human forms and etched drawings on articles such as needle cases are common. It has been suggested that these art objects served a magico-religious function, perhaps as charms or amulets, and were probably associated with shamanism.

A rare glimpse of one aspect of Dorset culture is provided by some sites in Baffinland, where the frozen ground has preserved the wooden artifacts. Among the items recovered are handles for stone tools (some with the stone blades still lashed in place), sled runners, harpoon foreshafts, and full-sized shaman masks.

Archaeologists are confronted with many problems regarding the Dorset people. Already mentioned is the nearly two thousand year hiatus between the Pre-Dorset and Dorset occupations of the eastern coast of Hudson Bay. Why did the apparently large and stable Dorset population on the island of Newfoundland (and presumably adjacent Quebec) disappear more than 500 years ago? There are a number of hypotheses, but none are convincing.

**Plate 22. The Dorset Stone Burial-vault** The first Dorset burial to be discovered was found in this large stone burial-vault. The body was laid on the ground and surrounded by large boulders, which were then roofed with flat rock slabs. An analysis of the skeletal remains indicated that the Dorset people were of a racial stock similar to present-day Inuit. However, some archaeologists believe this to be a Thule grave.

The fate of the late Dorset peoples of the northern and western coasts of Quebec, however, is clear. Sometime between the thirteenth and fifteenth centuries their culture was eradicated by an invading culture from the west — the Thule.

## Thule Culture

The Thule people were the forefathers of the present Inuit populations of Canada and Greenland. About A.D. 900 they spread east from their northern Alaskan homeland. A sea-mammal hunting technology permitted them to exploit the enormous baleen whales of the arctic waters. In less than 400 years they had

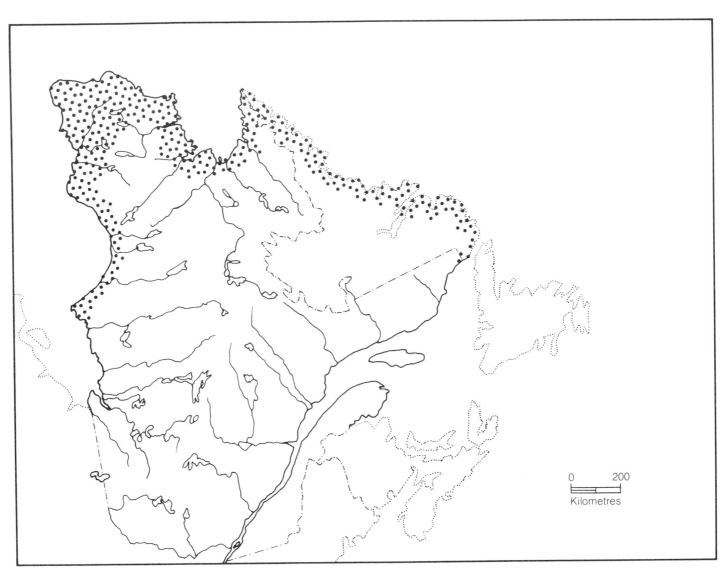

**Map 9. Distribution of the Thule Culture**

**Figure 17. Thule House Floor Plan**
The typical Thule (Inuit) winter house
was constructed from large rock slabs
and whale bone, which would have
been covered with sod. Such houses
usually have a raised sleeping
platform, a floor, and a narrow
passageway. Large soapstone lamps,
used for light, heat and cooking, are
often found in the pantry area. This
particular house was excavated in the
Northwest Territories, but comparable
structures have been reported from
northern Quebec.

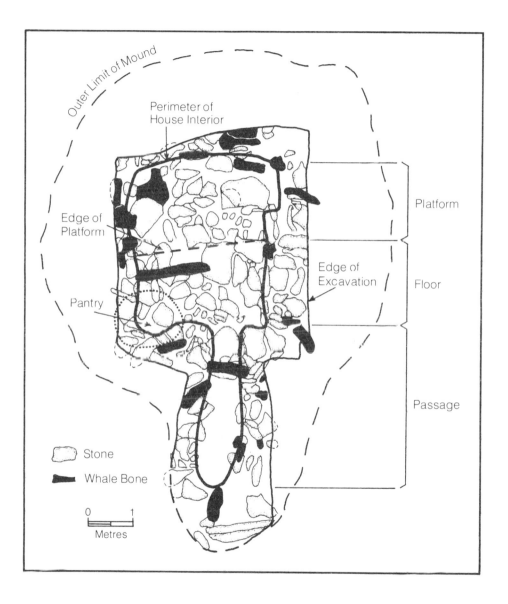

Outer Limit of Mound

Perimeter of
House Interior

Edge of
Platform

Platform

Edge of
Excavation

Floor

Pantry

Passage

☐ Stone

◣ Whale Bone

0        1

Metres

a     b     c

d     e     f

g

h     i

## Plate 23. Thule Artifacts

**a.** Barbed harpoon heads.

**b.** On the left is an ivory toggling harpoon head with an iron blade and rivet; on the right is a lateral view of a similar type of harpoon showing how the flat iron or stone blade fitted into the end of the harpoon.

**c.** Stone harpoon blades; the two on the right have been drilled to rivet the blade to the harpoon.

**d.** A barbed bone point, which may have been part of a fish or bird spear.

**e.** Wooden figure, possibly a doll.

**f.** An ulu; the bone handle above it has been separated from the ground-slate blade.

**g.** Ivory snow knife.

**h.** Soapstone pot with holes drilled in all four corners for suspension.

**i.** Bone arrowheads.

occupied most of arctic Canada and Greenland, and in the process replaced the late Palaeo-Eskimo Dorset people whose ancestors had inhabited the area for nearly 3500 years. There is no strong evidence to suggest that the Dorset women were absorbed by the Thule culture. If the Thule practised the same warfare pattern as their kinsmen who remained in Alaska, no quarter was given to enemies — men, women or children. If the Thule pushed the Palaeo-Eskimos out of the favourable hunting locations into marginal areas, they would eventually have starved. Nevertheless, some Thule and Dorset communities were contemporaneous in northern Quebec and along the eastern coast of Hudson Bay between the thirteenth and fifteenth centuries. But if cultural absorption, rather than annihilation, did take place during this period, it did so in a manner that has yet to be recognized by archeologists.

Shortly before European contact, the Thule had occupied the eastern coast of Hudson Bay to its juncture with James Bay, all of the northern Quebec coast, and part of the Labrador coast. In historic times, they expanded farther down the coast of Labrador and penetrated the north shore of the Gulf of St. Lawrence in Quebec. The combined attacks of the Montagnais and Micmac may have forced them to withdraw to the Labrador coast. Their descendants, the Inuit, still occupy the lands they wrested from the Palaeo-Eskimos.

The Thule culture was basically the same as the Inuit culture contacted by the Europeans between the sixteenth and nineteenth centuries. A major exception was the discontinuance of big-whale hunting, which had played an important part in Thule culture. It appears that changing ice conditions eventually forced the large whales out of range of the whaler's harpoon.

During the whaling era of the Thule culture, substantial winter villages were established at favourable locations. The houses were generally circular, semisubterranean structures with long,

**Plate 24. Stone Cairns** The *inuksuit* are stone cairns arranged in a pattern to lure caribou towards the waiting hunters. They were constructed by the late-prehistoric and historic Inuit, and dot the landscape in favoured caribou-hunting areas.

enclosed entrance-ways that faced the sea. An elevated sleeping platform was erected at the back of each house, and the floor was paved with carefully fitted flagstones. Large whalebone ribs and jaws were used to support the blocks of sod that served as the walls and roof. A pantry area, where a large soapstone lamp burned seal oil to provide heat, light and a means of cooking, was located in one corner of the house. In contrast, summer shelters were simple tents made of skin that was supported by wooden poles and held down by a ring of stones.

**Plate 25. Ungava Cairns** The great stone cairns of the Island of Ivik in the Ungava region are thought to have functioned as navigational aids, although they may have served other purposes. It is not known who constructed them — Dorset people, later Inuit, or, as has been suggested, Norsemen.

After the large-whale era, the Thule people concentrated on hunting seal, which were harpooned along the edge of the sea ice or caught by the *mapok* technique (the hunter harpooned the seal when it came up for air at its breathing hole in the ice). Other hunting undertaken during the various seasons of the year ranged from the pursuit of dangerous large animals such as walrus and polar bear, to the less hazardous stalking of caribou, the gathering of bird eggs and moulting birds, and the capture of spawning char in stone traps.

a     b

c

d

e

DdGt-5
2122

f

g

h

**Plate 26. Historic Period Trade Goods**

**a.** French flintlock mechanism with gunflint.

**b.** Metal arrowheads; the iron specimen on the left is of European manufacture, and the two on the right were produced by natives from discarded brass kettles.

**c.** Iron spearhead of European manufacture.

**d.** The iron axe above belongs to the French régime. The axe below is a ceremonial axe of the English period, which, with a pipe bowl on the butt end, also served as a pipe. The wooden handle would have doubled as a pipe stem.

**e.** European trade beads typical of the English period. The catalogue number on the card identifies the site and indicates where the beads were found in the excavation.

**f.** Iron strike-a-light used for starting fires by striking the iron against a flint to produce a spark.

**g.** Soapstone pipe bowl of the historic period.

**h.** An Inuit pipe with a wooden stem and an ornamental string of beads that prevented the pipe from breaking should it fall off the stem.

The technology of the Thule and their Inuit descendants was ideally adapted for exploiting the arctic environment. Their watercraft consisted of the umiak, a large skin boat, and the one-man kayak. A sled pulled by teams of large dogs was used for transport over land and ice. Hunting equipment consisted of the toggle-head harpoon with attached floats for hunting sea mammals; the bow and arrow for caribou; the lance for caribou and bear and for despatching small whales and walruses after they had been harpooned; the leister, a three-pronged fish spear; darts for birds; and many other devices. Harpoons and spears were often thrown with greater force by the use of a throwing board. Snow goggles were used to prevent snow-blindness, sleeping mattresses were made from woven baleen, a fibrous material obtained from the mouths of certain species of large whales, and fine tailored skin clothing was made with eyed bone and ivory needles. The list of objects archaeologists dig up is almost endless, and it is often difficult to determine what many of them were used for. The older Inuit, however, still recall the functions of many of their ancestors' tools.

One of the distinctive characteristics of Thule culture was the use of ground slate to make knives and tips for the ends of harpoons. The chipping of stone tools, so characteristic of the Palaeo-Eskimos, was rarely practised in Thule culture. Another Thule trait was the use of large boulders to construct houses, caches, graves, kayak stands, the ubiquitous *inuksuit* used to assist in the caribou hunt, and the *saput* used to channel migrating char into restricted areas where they could be speared. To judge from the size of the boulders in some of these structures, there must have been competitions to see who could lift the largest boulder!

The Thule occupation of Quebec, like the Palaeo-Eskimo occupation, was restricted to the coastal regions. This was, of course, sensible for a basically maritime culture, but in other regions of Canada Thule hunters made seasonal trips into the interior in search of caribou, which provided the best hides for clothing. Except in the northernmost parts of the province, such seasonal trips into the interior were probably blocked by Montagnais and Cree hunters.

The animosity between Inuit and Indian appears to have been of long standing, although today mixed communities live in harmony. Virtually no cultural borrowings are apparent between Inuit and Indian except for those initiated by European traders during the historic period, although the exchange of certain cultural traits would have been mutually beneficial. It can only be suggested that throughout the long period of their joint occupancy of the province, the culture, language and way of life of the Inuit and the Indian were so different that all contacts were viewed with suspicion. The historical records indicate that hostility dominated their relationship. This is probably why there appear to have been substantial buffer zones of unoccupied territory between them in the northern and western portions of Quebec.

# Epilogue

The area now represented by the province of Quebec has been occupied by man for approximately 11 000 years. Although the scattered camp debris and other vague evidence of prehistoric occupation that has accumulated over many thousands of years occurs in virtually all areas of the province, these remains are a limited and delicate resource; a resource menaced by the bulldozer blade and the rising flood waters of dams. Yet it is a unique resource, and once destroyed can never be replaced. The problem is brutally simple: any force, natural or man-made, that disturbs or buries the surface of the land is potentially destructive of prehistoric remains. The solution is not simple. Highways will continue to be built and dams constructed, cities and towns will expand, gravel and sand requirements will increase, and farmers will work their fields. The natural process of erosion will also continue. It is impractical to think that more than a small percentage of the prehistoric heritage can be preserved or salvaged in the face of such massive destruction. It is a practical goal, however, to develop vehicles for the preservation, investigation and interpretation of a sufficient portion of the province's prehistory to ensure that representative segments of that prehistory will not be obliterated. The Government of Quebec, through the Ministry of Cultural Affairs, and its agency, the Archaeological and Ethnological Service, has made laudable efforts, by means of legislation and salvage and inventory programmes, to preserve the prehistoric heritage of the province. Archaeologists require increased support by the public, however, if an essential portion of the province's prehistory is to be maintained for future generations.

For some people the fate of the prehistoric record is a matter of supreme indifference. There is similar unconcern about the threatened survival of certain animals, plants and birds. Fortunately, most people have an instinctive feeling that the past and the natural world should be studied and, where possible, protected. But they must hear the story that prehistory has to tell before they can make reasonable decisions regarding the development and preservation of yet another segment of their heritage. Archaeology possesses the capability of interpreting the past, but for how long? The unwritten pages of the past are being destroyed daily, never to be replaced.

This book has been written to provide the public with a glimpse of approximately 11 000 years of the human experience in the province of Quebec. It is a rich and fascinating story that is unfolding. But what has been written is an abstract; the chapters are still buried in the earth. Only action taken today will determine how many of those chapters will be read before they are lost forever.

# Appendix

## Archaeological Agencies

Archaeological excavations in Quebec are regulated by Bill 2 (Cultural Property Act), which received the assent of the National Assembly of Quebec in 1972. The Bill is administered by the Ministry of Cultural Affairs through its agency, the Archaeological and Ethnological Service. Queries should be addressed to:

Ministère des Affaires culturelles
Service d'archéologie et d'ethnologie
6, rue Université
Québec, Québec

The explanatory notes of Bill 2 outline the purpose and nature of the law:

*The main objects of this bill are to establish a Cultural Property Commission, to authorize the Minister of Cultural Affairs to recognize or classify cultural property, to provide for the regulation of excavations and archaeological surveys and to authorize the government to declare as a historic district a territory having a concentration of historic sites or monuments, or a natural district a territory whose natural setting presents an aesthetic, legendary or scenic interest.*

*The Cultural Property Commission will consist of twelve members appointed by the government; it will give its advice to the Minister on any question referred to it by him and on any question relating to the conservation of cultural property.*

*The Minister may, after taking the advice of the commission, recognize or classify any property or archaeological site the conservation of which is in the public interest. The cultural property so recognized may not be transported outside the province of Québec without the permission of the Minister; it may not be destroyed, altered or alienated without giving notice to the Minister; if offered for sale, he may acquire it by preference. If the property is classified, it must be kept in good condition; the permission of the Minister will be required to destroy, alter or alienate it; and, in the case of an immoveable, it may be exempt from real estate taxes up to half the value entered on the valuation roll.*

*The bill provides that to make archaeological excavations in the province of Québec it will now be necessary to obtain an archaeological research permit from the Minister; if made in an excavation or construction work undertaken for other than archaeological purposes, the Minister may order, subject to indemnity, the suspension for seven days of any work likely to compromise the property or site discovered. The government may, under the same conditions, extend such period to fifteen days and order a change of plans if the examination of the site reveals property which would have been classified if discovered before the start of the work.*

*In the parts of territory declared to be historic districts or natural districts, construction and sign-posting will be the object of a special regulation; any construction, repair or alteration of an immoveable must be authorized by the Minister unless the municipality where it is situated has adopted a building by-law in accordance with the standards determined by the government; the approval of the Minister will also be required for any exterior posting and any change of bill-boards.*

*The bill replaces the Historic Monuments Act (Revised Statutes, 1964, chapter 62) and other related acts.*


What can citizens who are concerned with preserving the province's prehistoric heritage do? They should inform the Archaeological and Ethnological Service in Quebec City if they have knowledge of archaeological collections or prehistoric sites and, in particular, if they know of archaeological sites in danger of destruction. The information may also be sent to one of the following institutions, which will pass the information on to the Archaeological and Ethnological Service:

## Montreal

Département d'anthropologie
Université de Montréal
Montréal, Québec

Department of Anthropology
McGill University
Montreal, Quebec

Laboratoire d'archéologie
Université du Québec à Montréal
Montréal, Québec

## Quebec

Département d'anthropologie
Université Laval
Québec, Québec

Centre d'Étude nordiques
Université Laval
Québec, Québec

## Trois-Rivières

Musée d'Archéologie préhistorique
Université du Québec à Trois-Rivières
Trois-Rivières, Québec

## Ottawa

Archaeological Survey of Canada
National Museum of Man
Ottawa, Ontario

# Glossary

**Abrader** An abrasive stone, such as sandstone, used to shape bone tools, to sharpen stone axes, and to do other tasks that involve a polishing or grinding action.

**Adze** A ground-stone woodworking tool, with the bit attached to the handle at right angles, like a hoe.

**Algonkian-speaking peoples** A widespread language family that includes such groups as the Micmac and Malecite of the Maritimes; the Montagnais, Cree, Algonkin and Ojibwa of the Shield; and the Blackfoot of the Plains. The Algonkin people of the Ottawa River watershed should not be confused with the language family. References to other language families, such as Iroquoian-speaking peoples, include equally diverse groups of people whose dialects were, to varying degrees, not mutually intelligible. They bear the same relation to one another as French, English, German or Spanish do in the Indo-European language family.

**Atlatl** An Aztec word referring to a spear-throwing board, which propelled a missile with greater force than was possible by hand.

**Awl** A sharply pointed tool, usually manufactured from bone but sometimes from copper, used for punching holes in leather and other materials in preparation for sewing or lashing.

**Axe** A ground-stone woodworking tool resembling a modern axe. It is different from an adze as it has a symmetrically bevelled bit rather than an asymmetrical one.

**Bayonet** A long, straight-sided lance or spear generally manufactured from slate that is ground (rather than chipped) into shape.

**Biface** A descriptive term applied to any chipped-stone artifact that has been shaped by removing flakes from both surfaces. Biface blade, for example, refers to tools that were used as knives.

**Celt** A general term used to describe a ground-stone woodworking tool that might have been hafted as either an adze or an axe.

**Champlain Sea** With the retreat of the continental glacier from what is now the St. Lawrence valley, the region was flooded by the ocean as a result of the higher sea levels of about 11 500 years ago. The gradually rising land, released from the enormous weight of the glacial ice, brought the Champlain Sea to an end sometime before 9000 years ago. Seal, whale, capelin, barnacles and other evidence of marine life from the Champlain Sea have been found in deposits as far inland as the upper Ottawa River valley.

**Core** A specifically shaped block of silica-rich stone from which flakes or blades are detached with a hammerstone or punch.

**Eskimo** *See* Inuit.

**Feature** Anything that the archaeologist can recognize in an excavation. A garbage dump, a cluster of post moulds, a pit or a concentration of tools are all examples of features.

**Flint** A term used to cover a wide variety of stones composed of nearly pure silica: chert is used in a similarly loose fashion. The glass-like properties of flint were ideally suited for manufacturing tools by chipping.

**Gouge** A woodworking tool, usually of polished stone, with a concave face at the bit end; similar to modern steel gouges.

**Gorge** A double-pointed object, usually of bone, attached at its centre to a fishing line and baited. When swallowed by a fish, it would lodge in the throat or stomach.

**Gorget** A polished stone pendant, usually of slate, with one or more drilled holes for suspension.

**Graphite** A black carbon, widely used as a pigment.

**Hammerstone** Any hard stone, usually a natural cobble, that exhibits evidence of having been used to strike flakes from other stones being fashioned into tools.

**Hearth** Any feature that presents evidence of having been used for a fire. It may be merely an area where a fire has oxidized the iron in the sand and turned it red or a large pit filled with fire-cracked rock.

**Hematite** *See* Ochre.

**Historic period** Refers to the period when Europeans were making written observations about the native peoples and lands they visited in the sixteenth and seventeenth centuries.

**Index fossil** Any tool that has sufficient characteristics to identify the culture and the approximate time period to which it belongs. Examples of index fossils are the fluted projectile points of the Clovis culture and the atlatl weights of the Laurentian culture.

**Inuksuit** An Inuit word for the stone piles that were used to lure caribou within shooting range. It means "like a man."

**Inuit** The majority of people who are commonly called *Eskimos* prefer the name *Inuit*. The word is derived from *inuk*, which means "man." Both terms, as applied in the text, refer to the same people.

**Iron pyrites** Nodules of this naturally-occurring iron sulphide are used with flint as part of a fire-making kit.

**Jasper** A general term referring to red, yellow and brown flints; the colours are the result of iron oxides in the silica.

**Leister** A specialized fish spear with a central prong and two lateral barbed prongs of bone or antler that grasp the fish on both sides after it has been struck.

**Native copper** Copper that occurs in a nearly pure state and does not require smelting.

**Ochre** Another name for hematite, a hydrated oxide of iron, which was widely used for painting objects and for sprinkling over the body of the deceased.

**Paintstone** Any natural stone, such as ochre or graphite, from which pigment can be obtained for the purpose of painting objects.

**Pit** Any hole dug into the ground. This would include holes for garbage or storage, excavated house floors and burials.

**Plummet** A small, generally egg-shaped stone that is grooved, or sometimes notched, at one end for suspension. Its function is uncertain.

**Post mould** When a wooden post rots away or is pulled out of the ground, the black surface soil fills the hole left by the post, leaving a black mould of the post's diameter, depth and angle in the yellow subsoil.

**Quartzite** A variety of rock, distributed across much of Quebec, whose high silica content makes it an excellent flaking material from which to make a wide range of sharp tools.

**Radiocarbon dating** A dating method based on the fact that all living matter, plant and animal, absorbs carbon during its lifetime. Upon the death of the organism, the radioactive isotope (carbon 14) is released at a constant rate that can be measured to calculate the time of death in absolute years. For example, if a living tree was cut down and used for firewood 5000 years ago and the archaeologist recovered the charcoal, the resulting date, determined by the radiocarbon dating method, should be approximately 5000 years.

**Saput** A stone fishweir constructed to trap fish in a restricted area where they could be speared.

**Scraper** A stone flake chipped on one or more edges; used for working hides, bone and wood.

**Stratigraphy** Distinct and successive layers of any deposited material.

**Toggle harpoon** A weapon with a head that is detachable from the shaft. It derives its holding power by turning or toggling in the wound around a line attached near the centre of the weapon tip.

**Ulu** Also called a semi-lunar knife because of its semicircular shape, it was generally made of ground and polished slate. The convex edge of the tool was sharpened.

# Suggested Reading List

These recommended readings in Quebec prehistory are listed under the headings General, Indian Prehistory, and Palaeo-Eskimo and Inuit Prehistory. Indian prehistory is subdivided according to time period and cultural group.

In a number of instances, where publications dealing specifically with Quebec are not available, reports from adjacent provinces or states are recommended, as they reflect similar cultural developments. An attempt has been made to list only reports that have a broad scope or present a detailed examination of a major archaeological site. Additional references can be found in the bibliographies of the recommended books and articles.

## General

**Chapdelaine, Claude**
(1978) "Images de la préhistoire du Québec." *Recherches Amérindiennes au Québec* 7(1–2).

**Chevrier, Daniel**
(1977) *Préhistoire de la région de la Moisie.* Cahiers du Patrimoine 5. Québec: Ministère des Affaires culturelles, Service d'archéologie et d'ethnologie.

An interpretation of archaeological remains spanning a six thousand-year period in the Moisie River region on the north shore of the Gulf of St. Lawrence.

**Crête, Serge-André**
(1976) "Les Amérindiens" in *Histoire du Québec,* ed. Jean Hamelin, Toulouse: Édouard Privat, pp. 11–25.

A general outline of the prehistory of Quebec.

**Marois, Roger J. M.**
(1975) *L'archéologie des provinces de Québec et d'Ontario.* Musée national de l'Homme, Collection Mercure, Commission archéologique du Canada, dossier 44.

A description of archaeological research in Quebec and Ontario to 1968.

**Martijn, Charles**
(1974) "État de la recherche en préhistoire du Québec." *Revue de Géographie de Montréal* 28(4): 429–42.

A review of recent archaeological research in Quebec by region, and an outline of the major prehistoric periods.

**Martijn, Charles A., and Cinq-Mars, Jacques**
(1970) "Aperçu sur la recherche préhistorique au Québec." *Revue de Géographie de Montréal* 24(2): 175–88.

A review of prehistoric research in Quebec and Labrador, including a suggested policy to promote the development of prehistoric studies in the province.

**Taylor, William E., Jr.**
(1964) *The Prehistory of the Quebec-Labrador Peninsula.* Paris: École pratique des hautes études, Bibliothèque arctique et antarctique 2.

*La préhistoire de la péninsule du Labrador.* Musée national du Canada, Études anthropologiques 7.

English and French summaries, prepared in 1961, of the prehistory of the area to the north of a base line drawn from Moosonee to Tadoussac.

## General Studies in Areas Adjacent to Quebec

**McGhee, Robert**
(1976) *The Burial at L'Anse-Amour.* Ottawa: National Museums of Canada.

An imaginative reconstruction of events that may have led to the construction of a Maritime Archaic burial mound on the south Labrador coast 7500 years ago, followed by a description of what was actually found during the archaeological excavation.

(1978) *Canadian Arctic Prehistory*. Scarborough, Ont.: Van Nostrand Reinhold for the National Museum of Man, National Museums of Canada.
 A synthesis of Canadian Arctic prehistory intended for the general reader; includes the prehistory of northern Quebec.

**Ritchie, William A.**
(1965) *The Archaeology of New York State*. Garden City, N.Y.: Natural History Press.
 A detailed study of the prehistory of New York State. Many of the developments that took place in New York prehistory are similar to those in southern Quebec.

**Tuck, James A.**
(1976) *Newfoundland and Labrador Prehistory*. Scarborough, Ont.: Van Nostrand Reinhold for the National Museum of Man, National Museums of Canada.
 A synthesis of Newfoundland prehistory intended for the general reader; pertinent to the Gulf of St. Lawrence of Quebec.

**Wright, J. V.**
(1972) *Ontario Prehistory, An Eleven-Thousand-Year Archaeological Outline*. Scarborough, Ont.: Van Nostrand Reinhold for the National Museum of Man, National Museums of Canada.
 A synthesis of Ontario prehistory intended for the general reader; pertinent to the prehistory of western and southern Quebec.

(1976) *Six Chapters of Canada's Prehistory*. Scarborough, Ont.: Van Nostrand Reinhold for the National Museum of Man, National Museums of Canada.

 Intended for the general reader, this is a general examination of six aspects of prehistory (hunting, fishing, farming, toolmaking, trading, and housing); includes elements from the prehistory of Quebec.

# Indian Prehistory

## Palaeo-Indian Period

**Benmouyal, Joseph**
(1976) "Archaeological Research in the Gaspé Peninsula, Preliminary Report." *Current Research Reports* 3: 7–18. Burnaby, B.C.: Simon Fraser University, Department of Archaeology.
 A short description of Palaeo-Indian (Plano) material from the Gaspé and of later cultural remains.

**MacDonald, George F.**
(1968) *Debert: A Palaeo-Indian Site in Central Nova Scotia*. National Museum of Canada Anthropology Paper 16.
 A detailed description of a Palaeo-Indian (Clovis) site.

## Archaic Period

**Clermont, Norman**
(1974) "Un site archaïque de la région de Chambly." *Recherches amérindiennes au Québec* 4(3): 34–51.
 A description of a Laurentian autumn fishing campsite located on the Richelieu River.

**Kennedy, Clyde C.**
(1967) "Preliminary Report on the Morrison's Island-6 Site." Contributions to Anthropology V. *National Museum of Canada Bulletin* 206: 100–125.

A description of a Laurentian Archaic campsite and cemetery located on an island in the Ottawa River.

**Marois, Roger J.M., and Ribes, René**
(1975) *Indices de manifestations culturelles de l'archaïque: la région de Trois-Rivières.* Musée national de l'Homme, Collection Mercure, Commission archéologique du Canada, dossier 41.

This study examines the evidence for contact between Laurentian Archaic and Maritime Archaic peoples in the region of Trois-Rivières.

**Martijn, Charles A., and Rogers, Edward S.**
(1969) *Mistassini–Albanel: Contributions to the Prehistory of Québec.* Centre d'Études nordiques 25. Québec: université Laval.

A detailed description of the predominantly Shield Archaic materials recovered from the Mistassini-Albanel region of south-central Quebec, and an examination of the way of life of the present-day Cree occupants.

**McGhee, Robert, and Tuck, James A.**
(1975) *An Archaic Sequence from the Strait of Belle Isle, Labrador.* National Museum of Man, Mercury Series, Archaeological Survey of Canada Paper 34.

A detailed description of the Maritime Archaic cultural sequence along the south Labrador coast, which is related to developments on the north shore of the Gulf of St. Lawrence.

**Tuck, James A.**
(1975) *Prehistory of Saglek Bay, Labrador: Archaic and Palaeo-Eskimo Occupations.* National Museum of Man, Mercury Series, Archaeological Survey of Canada Paper 32.

A description of the late Maritime Archaic, early Palaeo-Eskimo and Dorset occupations of northern Labrador, which are related to archaeological developments both on the north coast of Quebec and along the Gulf of St. Lawrence.

**Wright, J.V.**
(1972) *The Shield Archaic.* National Museum of Man, Publications in Archaeology 3.

A detailed description of the Shield Archaic, including sites in Quebec.

## Initial Woodland Period

**Clermont, Norman**
(1976) "Un site du sylvicole inférieur à Sillery." *Recherches amérindiennes au Québec* 6(1): 37–44.

A description and interpretation of an early Woodland grave found during road construction at Quebec City.

**Lévesque, René; Osborne, Fitz; and Wright, J.V.**
(1964) *Le gisement de Batiscan.* Musée national du Canada, Études anthropologiques 6.

A report on a Meadowood campsite.

**Mitchell, Barry M.**
(1966) *Preliminary Report on a Woodland Site near Deep River, Ontario.* National Museum of Canada Anthropology Papers 11.

A description of a predominantly Point Peninsula site. Historic materials are also described.

# Terminal Woodland Period

THE ST. LAWRENCE IROQUOIS

### Direction générale du Patrimoine
(1975) *Mandeville, site archéologique préhistorique.*
Québec: Ministère des Affaires culturelles, Service
d'archaéologie et d'ethnologie, dossier 2.

A brief and general description of a St. Lawrence
Iroquois site located on the Richelieu River near its
juncture with the St. Lawrence River. The document
was prepared to help secure protection for the site
under Bill 2 of the province of Quebec.

### Girouard, Laurent
(1975) *Station 2, Pointe-aux-Buissons.* Cahiers du Patrimoine 2. Québec: Ministère des Affaires culturelles,
Service d'archéologie et d'ethnologie.

A detailed description of a St. Lawrence Iroquois
fishing camp on the St. Lawrence River, with particular
emphasis on the analysis of ceramics.

### Pendergast, James F.
(1967) "The Berry Site." *National Museum of Canada
Bulletin* 206: 26–53.

A description of an early St. Lawrence Iroquois site
in southern Quebec.
(1975) "An In-situ Hypothesis to Explain the Origin of
the St. Lawrence Iroquoians."*Ontario Archaeology* 25:
47–55.

A working hypothesis that seeks to explain the origins of the Hochelagans and Stadaconans and where
they went after leaving their homeland along the St.
Lawrence River.

### Pendergast, James F., and Trigger, Bruce G.
(1972) *Cartier's Hochelaga and the Dawson Site.*
Montreal: McGill-Queen's University Press.

A detailed archaeological and ethnohistoric examination of a historic St. Lawrence Iroquois site in
Montreal.

THE ALGONKIN

### Marois, Roger J. M.
(1974) *Les schèmes d'établissement à la fin de la
préhistoire et au début de la période historique: le sud
du Québec.* Musée national de l'Homme, Collection
Mercure, Commission archéologique du Canada,
dossier 17.

A geographical study of the location in southern
Quebec of the Algonkian-speaking bands of the sixteenth and seventeenth centuries, with archaeological
data from Lake Abitibi and from west of the Gatineau
River to support certain theoretical considerations. A
good résumé of the historical documents.

THE MONTAGNAIS

### Lévesque, René
(1971) *La seigneurie des îles et des îlots de Mingan.*
Archéologie du Québec. Ottawa: Leméac.

A description of a stratified Montagnais site located
by accident during the excavation of a trading post
constructed by Louis Jolliet in 1680.

THE MICMAC-MALECITE

### Barré, Georges
(1975) *Cap-Chat (DgDq-1), un site du sylvicole moyen
en Gaspésie.* Cahiers du Patrimoine 1. Québec: Ministère des Affaires culturelles, Service d'archéologie et
d'ethnologie.

A description of a stratified sixth-to-seventh-century
Micmac–Malecite campsite. The ethnic identification is
mine rather than Mr. Barré's.

# Palaeo-Eskimo and Inuit Prehistory

**Barré, Georges**
(1970) *Reconnaissance archéologique dans la région de la baie de Wakeham (Nouveau-Québec).* Montréal: Société d'archéologie préhistorique du Québec.

A description of Dorset and Thule cultures and historic Inuit sites in the Ungava region.

**Hartweg, Raoul, and Plumet, Patrick**
(1974) *Archéologie du Nouveau-Québec: sépultures et squelettes de l'Ungava.* Collection Paléo-Québec 3. Montréal: Laboratoire d'archéologie de l'université du Québec.

An archaeological and physical-anthropological description of Palaeo-Eskimo and Inuit graves and skeletal remains from Ungava.

**Taylor, W. E., Jr.**
(1968) *The Arnapik and Tyara Sites.* Society for American Archaeology Memoirs 22.

A major study of the origins and nature of Dorset culture in the eastern Canadian Arctic, northern Quebec, and Greenland from between 800 B.C. and A.D. 1300.

# Miscellaneous

### Cahiers d'Archéologie québécoise
(1969) *Le musée d'Archéologie, le centre des Études universitaires de Trois-Rivières.*

The two articles in this volume are entitled "Recherches archéologiques dans la région du Grand Lac Meckinac" by René Ribes, and "Île-aux-Basques and the Prehistoric Iroquois Occupation of Southern Quebec" by Charles A. Martijn.

**Marois, Roger J. M.**
(1972) *Vocabulaire français-anglais, anglais-français d'archéologie préhistorique.* Montréal: Presses de l'Université du Québec.

This vocabulary lists a number of technical archaeological terms, and attempts to arrive at a consistent usage in both French and English.
(1975) *Quelques techniques de décoration de la céramique impressionnée: correspondance des termes français et anglais.* Musée national de l'Homme, Collection Mercure, Commission archéologique du Canada, dossier 40.

This study examines ceramic description in French and English archaeological reports, and determines where such descriptions do or do not correspond.

**Tassé, Gilles, and Dewdney, Selwyn**
(1977) *Relevés et travaux récents sur l'art rupestre amérindien.* Collection Paléo-Québec 8. Montréal: Laboratoire d'archéologie de l'Université du Québec.

A number of aspects of native rock paintings are considered in this study with emphasis on petroglyph sites in southwestern Quebec.

The following serials contain articles or monographs describing various aspects of Quebec prehistory:
*Cahiers d'archéologie québécoise.* Trois-Rivières, Qué.: Musée d'Archéologie.
*Cahiers du Patrimoine* and *Dossier.* Québec: Ministère des Affaires culturelles, Service d'archéologie et d'ethnologie.
*Centre d'Études nordiques, Travaux et documents.* Québec: Presses de l'université Laval.
*Collection Paléo-Québec.* Trois-Rivières, Qué.: Université du Québec.
*Recherches amérindiennes au Québec, Bulletin d'information.* Montréal.
*Société d'Archéologie du Saguenay.* Occasional publications. Chicoutimi, Qué.

# Index